Anchor Cove

Toni Shiloh

Cover design by Toni Shiloh.

Cover art photos © Depositphotos.com/MartyInkTank (Martins Ozols) and Aquiro14b (Zdenek Bohm) used by permission.

Edited by Marginalia Editing.

Published in the United States of America by Toni Shiloh.

www.ToniShiloh.com

Anchor Cove is a work of fiction. Names, characters, places, and incidents are either products of the author's imagination or used fictitiously. All characters are fictional, and any similarity to people living or dead is purely coincidental.

Formatted with Vellum

Dedication

To the Author and Finisher of my faith.

Chapter One

Derrick

TWENTY YEARS OF MY LIFE GIVEN TO THE UNITED STATES Air Force, and with God's prompting, I'd turned in my retirement papers. From the moment I enlisted until I retired last week, my life has been very much like the tide of the ocean. It knows when to rise, it knows when to recede. But now my military routine no longer exists. At thirty-eight, I'm not really sure what to do with myself.

Water meets the sand, falls back, then repeats the pattern across the shore as a cool ocean breeze fans me. I breathe in the salt air, trying to find the peace that's evaded me since I donned my uniform for the last time. My stomach churns like a Class 4 rapid.

Where are You? What do You want me to do next?

After what had been an obvious call for me to retire, God has gone radio silent. The nonstop quiet from Him makes me wonder if maybe I misheard Him in the first place.

I stare into the overcast sky.

Where are You, Lord? Why won't You answer me?

But silence greets my ears.

My jaw clenches, and my hands ball into fists. Why do I

expect now to be any different? He hasn't spoken to me in a few months. I have no choice but to figure out my next steps by myself.

I turn away from the surf and head toward the boardwalk. When I first parked at the beach, I thought some time in front of the ocean would bring peace. After all, that's the very reason for choosing to spend my summer in the coastal town of Anchor Cove, Maryland.

Should've known that would be too good to be true.

Nothing seems to be going my way.

My cell chimes with an incoming notification, so I tap the rental app to read a message from my new landlord. The beach house I'm renting for the summer is now ready for me to move into. Thanks to a military retirement check and savings I've accrued over the years, I don't need to rush to find another job. Yet I *want* direction. *Any* direction.

For now, checking into my temporary home then finding something to eat are my next steps. I get into my Jeep and plug the rental address into the GPS. The automated voice directs me to a yellow two-story home on stilts. The foundation isn't raised very high—a couple of feet off the ground—and matches the other brightly painted houses, giving off a tropical vibe. Too bad the cheery yellow isn't a morose gray to fit my mood.

With a sigh, I grab my two military-issued duffel bags and carry them up the stairs. After I punch the six-digit pin into the keypad deadbolt, the door handle flashes green and unlocks. Dead quiet greets me.

No air conditioner whirls. No TV plays. No sounds of aircraft taking off overhead. I'm definitely not on a military base anymore. A loop around the house ensures everything is in working order. I haven't met the landlord personally, but it appears she does a good job of maintaining her rental property. She encouraged me to reach out whenever I need something, but judging from the quick inspection, I won't have to speak to her or anyone else.

Just the way I want it.

The primary room holds an empty closet, providing space for the few dress shirts I own. My T-shirts are folded like I learned in basic training and easily slide into the chest of drawers. I make quick work of unpacking my clothing. Anchor Cove's dress code involves shorts, T-shirts, and flip flops—though I prefer wearing a pair of Jordans.

I sink onto the bed and open my saved websites on my cell phone. Before coming out here, I scoped out all the eateries within a mile radius of the beach house. Scrolling through the places, a restaurant called Oasis shows *open* as their current status. The pictures of the food look on point. This place is located in someone's backyard a block away. The pictures give a relaxing vibe and seem a bit isolated as well. Right up my alley. But if my stomach continues to grumble, it won't matter who's around so long as I get a decent meal.

Grabbing my wallet and cell, I slip them into my two back pockets. Traveling through the neighborhood is easy enough and I quickly find the blue-stilted home. A driftwood sign labeled Oasis decorates the front lawn. Since it's on the left side, I veer off in that direction. Judging from the amount of noise, the backyard hideaway entrance is on this side. A pebbled path appears, leading me to a hostess podium guarding the back entrance.

"Welcome to the Oasis. Table for one?" The hostess welcomes me with a smile.

"Yes, ma'am."

Her nose crinkles at the honorific but I don't have the heart to tell the twenty-something-year-old that every woman is *ma'am* and every man *sir*, no matter their age. Military service ingrained manners into my vocabulary.

I follow her around the corner and pause at the sight before me. A green-blue boat stands in the very back serving as a makeshift bar. Tall, green hedges close the entire space, but they don't create a suffocating space. Not with the white lights creating a relaxing atmosphere that immediately puts me at ease.

The hostess seats me at a wooden table for one, complete with its very own chair. Not two but one. People really can eat here without being pestered or made to feel awkward eating by themselves. I read that in the reviews but forgot until now. A server takes my drink and meal order then leaves me alone.

I'm no stranger to solitude and prefer it to nonsensical conversation. But since the Lord has stopped speaking to me, silence has felt like punishment. Not to mention, being left with only your thoughts when you'd rather focus on anything but makes my insides unsteady.

My burger and fries arrive, allowing me to focus on filling my stomach and shutting off my brain. A few bites in, it becomes quite obvious my thoughts refuse to stay hidden.

What's the plan? What are you going to do when summer ends?

Twenty years of always having *the plan* plus contingencies means being without one is akin to walking without a flashlight in the dark. I don't want to stumble my way through and merely pray I don't get hurt. Despite feeling enshrouded in the darkness these last few months, my vision still hasn't adjusted.

You don't have to figure out anything today.

The whole summer lies before me. I've allotted the entire one-hundred-and-four days of summer vacation to come up with a new life plan. Sure, the deadline is self-imposed, but I thrive on setting goals.

God, please talk to me before then. Please.

Hasn't the silence gone on long enough? I submitted my retirement paperwork four months ago. Out of all my friends who enlisted the same year as me, I'm the only one without a job lined up. Sure, I had interviews, but none of the jobs felt right. And none of them were green-lit by God.

Thankfully, my mom recommended I get away and unwind. Coming to Anchor Cove has been the only thing that's felt right since I retired. That doesn't mean I still don't want to crawl out of my skin. From youth, I've always thrived on routine, and I miss having one desperately.

It's okay to relax. It's okay to unwind.

But instead of giving me peace, the affirmations only widen the gulf between me and the Lord. I'm adrift without an anchor. Unmoored so easily as the discharge papers personnel handed me before I left my very last base.

I push my food away, no longer hungry. Day one and I'm already failing the relax and unwind mantra Mom encouraged me to adhere to.

God, I sure do hope You have a plan for me here.

Because I don't know how much more of the silence I can bear.

Simone

"Taj, let's go!" I shout up the stairs.

My son is never ready on time. At fifteen, he moves to the beat of his own drum and no matter how fast I try to speed him up, he never varies from his internal rhythm.

"I'm coming."

"You need to move a little faster. Aren't you supposed to be there at six?" I check my watch for the umpteenth time.

Though Anchor Cove is small—the inlet's about five square miles—it still takes a little time to drive from one end to the other thanks to the copious amounts of stoplights and tourist traffic that has arrived this Memorial weekend.

Taj descends the steps and sighs. "Mom, no one is on time to these things. I keep telling you that."

The broody look on his handsome face about does me in. How is he fifteen? How did we get here so fast? In the beginning, parenting took every single thing within me. Now we have a rhythm that's only disrupted by his bouts of moodiness or my I'm-a-bad-mom chocolate-eating meltdowns.

"Just because your friends show up late, doesn't mean you have to. I'm sure Misha will appreciate your punctuality."

"Ugh. Do you realize how old you sound?"

"Excuse me, sir. I'm not even in my mid-thirties." Considering I had him a couple of weeks after I turned eighteen, I'm a baby compared to his friends' parents.

"Yeah, well, you were born in the 1900s."

"Go." I point toward the front door, barely containing my laughter. This kid is too much.

He smirks, fully aware I find him amusing. But seriously, do I *look* like I'm from the last century?

Maybe I need to change my skincare routine.

We get in my black sedan as I head for the other side of Anchor Cove where Misha's having her sweet sixteen party. The two go to youth group together. Taj would never admit it, but the crush he harbors on Misha runs deep. Pretty sure she invited the entire youth group though, not just Taj.

I glance at him. "Did you grab the gift?"

"Yes, Mom." He raises the box he wrapped on his own.

"You've asked me like a hundred times and saw me walk out of the house with it."

Not a bad job.

"Right." Sometimes my brain melts down before the sun sets. Remembering everything I need to accomplish along with keeping track of another human life takes a lot of brain power. No one tells you caring for others will slowly decrease your own cognition. If only I'd known.

You wouldn't trade Taj for all the brain power in the world.

I sigh and sneak a peek at my sweet baby boy.

"You're staring again," he mumbles.

"I can't help it. Do you know how much I love you?"

His head flops back. "Yes. You tell me often."

"Yes, but do you *know?*"

Silence meets my ears. I focus on the road but really, my mind's totally focused on my son. In three years' time, he'll graduate from high school and fly the coop. What am I going to do without him in my life? Yes, I have to sever the apron strings, but I'd rather double knot them and add some high-powered glue. Then he'd be by my side forever.

You can't stifle him, Simone. You've got to let him grow into a man.

So much easier said than done.

"Call me when you need to be picked up." I park in front of the teen center. "*Call,* not text. I might not hear the notification of a message."

"Okay."

"Have fun. Tell Misha I said happy birthday."

Exasperation covers Taj's teen face. "Can I go now, Mom?"

"Bye, boy."

He grins. "Love you."

"Love you too." I really love that stinker.

He walks into the teen center, and I hold back a sigh. Now what? Taj will be occupied for the next few hours, and I have nothing to do. No properties to check on, no friends to talk to—they're all busy. I have nothing. No one.

Tears well in my eyes, but I draw in a deep breath to keep my thoughts from spiraling further. I'm *not* alone, just by myself at the moment. Since moving to Anchor Cove, I've built a great life for Taj and myself. We have friends so close we consider them family. Still, at the end of the day, it's just the two of us.

My stomach grumbles, sending my thoughts on a different trail. I could probably kill some time by eating dinner. But do I want to go home and make a meal or . . .

The Oasis pops into my mind and my lips curve. That's the perfect place to spend time waiting for Taj. Getting a table for one is easy and never awkward. Plus, they serve the most delectable food. Win-win.

I turn the car south and drive a couple of miles until an open parking spot frees up right across the street from the restaurant. Talk about good fortune. God must be smiling down on me and reminding me He's still with me even when I'm utterly alone.

Since Taj started high school last year, I've been battling bouts of loneliness. This fall he'll be a sophomore and I'm wholly unprepared for him to be halfway through high school. Time needs to slow down as soon as possible.

I walk around the back of the house to the backyard where Mrs. Meyer turned her spot into a true oasis. The gorgeous greenery always puts me at ease because she hedged in her yard, leaving the patrons with a private, secluded space. Single tables are placed here and there as well as tables for bigger parties. She welcomes any and everyone. If the yard overflows, then the few tables on her back deck keep the place from being too crowded. That, and she has no trouble turning people away when she meets fire safety capacity.

As I wait for a hostess, I scan the tables and note one other single person. My gaze pauses on the man. He doesn't look familiar so he's probably a tourist. He must have found the restaurant on one of those "hidden secrets of Anchor Cove" sites.

And who wouldn't love the Oasis? The white lights hanging from the slate balcony lend a cozy and intimate ambiance to the place. And there's something about the ash-blond tables and chairs that brighten up the area and balance against the greenery decor.

"Hey, Simone." Lacey steps up to the podium. "Just you?" She peeks around my shoulder as if searching for my son.

"Just me. Taj is at a party."

"Oh, cool. Right this way."

She leads me through the crowd and places me at a table right behind the stranger. I settle into my seat, trying not to stare at the back of his head. There's something about his presence that appears relaxed yet alert all at once. I wonder what his story is.

I like to play this game whenever I see a vacationer and ask myself what brought them to Anchor Cove. Will they find what they're looking for? Do they know the Lord?

At that thought, something stirs in my heart. It's a lot like that Holy Spirit nudge to pray.

But for what, Lord?

My gaze flies to the stranger in front of me. Is he okay? Did he arrive here weary from life? I bite my lip as the nudge grows stronger. I bow my head, closing my eyes.

Lord God, I'm not sure exactly what You want me to pray, but I pray for the man in front of me. I don't know who he is or what he's going through, but You do. Please bless his stay in Anchor Cove. May he find the answers to his questions. May You meet him in the process, and may You receive all the glory. Please keep him safe and bring rest to his soul. In Jesus's name, Amen.

I exhale as the nudge abates. The peace flooding my mind tells me that praying for this man was the right thing to do. I'm not sure exactly what his issues are, but I don't need to know. I've done my part and I can move on from this moment.

Though I'd still like to know what he's going through. I'm naturally curious, but at least I can be satisfied knowing I've done what the Lord asked of me.

You don't need to know the end result.

Besides, I have my own worries, my own answers I pray God will respond to in the near future. Until then, I'll try and enjoy life as best as I can.

Chapter Two

Derrick

I huff out breath after breath as I count out the push-ups that have been part of my morning routine for years. Even though my military service is complete, I can't stop twenty years of conditioning. Though nowadays my achy shoulder and bum knee stop me from going beyond my limits. It's a good thing I won't have to worry about passing the physical tests anymore.

Rolling onto my back, I move into sit-ups, trying to keep the *what-ifs* from intruding on my morning. But all I hear are the unanswered questions. What am I going to do now? I could probably find a civilian job equivalent to my Air Force career, but do I even want to? Does *God* want me to? I haven't been without a job since before I turned sixteen and started working at the local fast-food restaurant back home. Being without work makes me antsy enough I almost want to find the nearest recruiter's office. Surely they'll let me back in.

I exhale and lay on my back. Exercise isn't clearing my brain, so maybe a walk on the boardwalk will bring some quiet.

Please, Lord. I need my brain to shut off.

I used to be an expert on thinking about nothing. But ever since God made it clear I should retire, all I've focused on is tomorrow. A complete contradiction to God's Word on not worrying, but something my brain won't heed.

By the time I've walked the two blocks to the boardwalk, the tension in my shoulders has seeped out. I'm no longer amped from the workout, but my mind still isn't quiet either. The sound of the waves calls to me. It's better than any white noise machine.

I find a bench to sit on, then stare out onto the gray-blue waves. The sky's a bit overcast. Has my arrival brought the clouds? Anchor Cove is known for abundant sunshine in the summertime, but I haven't seen the big ball of gas yet.

A handful of teens playing volleyball nearby cheer. My gaze turns their way as they resume their game. Some of them are actually quite good, and others are obviously playing for pure enjoyment. They have no form or skill to speak of.

With all the crowds that will be descending on Anchor Cove, I'm hoping to slip under the radar and go unnoticed. I just want to reorient myself and figure out my next move without people hassling me.

My phone chimes and I pull the phone out of my shorts pocket and read the message from my mom.

MOM

Did you make it there safely?

If I don't reply, she'll track me down, even if that means notifying the police. Certainly wouldn't be the first time she's done something like that. It's better to handle her on my own terms.

Yes, ma'am.

MOM

Oh, good. Praying for you. I know the beach will be an answer to prayers.

How does she know that? *I* don't even fully believe I'll get the answers I desperately seek. I grimace. Doubt's an ugly word in my faith, but one that's been my constant companion these past four months. No matter how many times I pray, I can't shake my distrust. No matter how much Scripture I read that tells me God is trustworthy.

Having my plans altered has shaken my foundation. How do I correct it?

What do I do, Lord? Please *answer me.*

I wait. And wait. And wait.

Obviously, I won't be getting any answers today. I leave my spot on the bench and head back toward my rental. I need a shower and second breakfast. The protein shake I drank upon waking only saw me through my workout. Now my stomach demands a real meal.

As I walk past the colorful homes, a few people nod or greet me with a *good morning.* I dip my head each time, but irritation slowly creeps in. I'm not opposed to a friendly town, but being hungry and talking before I'm ready is a recipe for *hangry.* I head up the driveway of my rental and stop when I hear a groan coming from the teen the next driveway over.

He kicks the tire of the golf cart in the driveway. Judging from his tantrum, the thing won't start.

"Need some help?" I don't really want to get involved, but I won't leave a kid stranded either.

The teen freezes and stares at me. "Uh, no, sir. That's okay."

"I promise, I'm not a bad person." I hike a thumb over my shoulder. "I'm renting this place. I can show you my driver's license. Whatever makes you comfortable." I jerk my chin toward the golf cart. "Just wanted to know if I can help."

"Can you make a golf cart start?" The boy rubs the scruff growing on his chin.

I cross the grass between our two driveways. "Let's see what I can do." I turn the key. No clicking noise, so that's good. I head to the back and lift the panel up. A quick glance shows the battery isn't corroded.

"When's the last time you added water?" I ask.

"Huh? Water where?"

"You got any distilled water in your garage?"

"Let me check." He runs into the space, moving things around. He comes back out a moment later with a gallon jug. "Here it is."

I pour some in, then replace the cap. "Try and start it now."

The kids' brows rise, but he sits in the front and starts the golf cart without a hitch.

"Whoa. How did you know that?" He looks over his shoulder at me.

"I worked on a golf course before." It'd been miserable considering I wasn't a fan of the sport, but I'd learned some things.

"Awesome. Thanks, man." He holds out a fist.

I give him a dap. "No problem. Name's Derrick."

"I'm Taj."

"Nice to meet you. Feel free to come over if you ever need help again."

Why did you say that? He probably has a dad who could help out.

"I just might. My mom's busy right now or I would've called her for help."

Does that mean the kid *doesn't* have a dad around? *Don't be nosy.*

"See you around, kid." I wave, then jog up the steps to my rental.

As soon as I cross the threshold, the tension leaves my shoulders. Is it sad that being useful for a few minutes almost makes me want to smile? Should I get a summer job and stay busy around Anchor Cove?

No, that defeats the whole purpose of a vacation.

I rub the back of my neck as I enter the kitchen. Mom was right. Living a life that left little room for vacations means I don't know how to relax. Then again, it's the nature of the military to be ready for anything. Now I'm, what, just shooting the breeze until God speaks again?

Frustration runs through me. Why would God tell me to retire and then leave me on read for what comes next? Have I done something to upset Him?

There's no major sin in my life I can think of. At least, not any that hasn't already been repented of. I've done the necessary work to make sure I'm living for Him and not myself.

"Stop thinking," I say out loud. Maybe hearing my own voice will get my brain to quit with the questions already.

I crack some eggs into the skillet then use the spatula to mix everything. After the eggs have been scrambled, I slide them onto a plate and add two pieces of buttered toast. My water bottle is already full, so I grab it and sit at the breakfast table. I look out the window in the kitchen that gives a view of the backyard. There's a hammock tied to the trees waiting for me. If I practice doing nothing, perhaps I'll learn what true rest looks like.

Here's hoping.

Simone

I stare in dismay at the water pooling in the kitchen and living room. The security deposit I charged for this place will *not* cover the flooding the tenants left behind. I want to cry, but there's no time for that. This water needs to get sucked up and dried out before something worse happens.

Unfortunately, I won't be able to tell how bad the damage is until I get the flood waters out and the tile dried. I can only pray the flooring won't have to be replaced. That would cost a pretty penny.

And that's why you have an emergency fund.

Still, if the tenants hadn't flooded the dishwasher, this wouldn't have happened.

A knock sounds at the front.

"Come in!" I yell. I slosh through the water in my rain boots. "Be careful. There's a lot of water."

I don't need an injury lawsuit on top of all this.

Lewis, the local plumber, walks in. "Heard you had a leak, not a flood." His mouth drops at the amount of water.

I snort. "Good news travels fast, I see."

"Let me have a look. You know where it's coming from?"

"Dishwasher." I point to the offender. "I turned it off. It was the only thing running when I got here."

A local business owner had been walking their dog and noticed water pouring down the front steps. Not a call I'd been happy to receive. I place a hand to my forehead, trying to hold back the tears.

"Gotcha. Let's have a look."

Lewis kneels on one knee, opening the dishwasher. He breaks out his flashlight, peering into the nooks and crannies.

I'm not sure what he's looking for, but when he says, "Aha," my heart stutters to a stop.

"What is it?"

"Looks like they used too much rinse aid. Went on down and interfered with the gasket seal." Lewis shakes his head. "Recipe for flooding."

"I will remove every single rinse aid from every property pronto."

He chuckles. "Nah, you don't need to do that. Heard you had teens in here. That's all that is."

My policy says twenty-one and up, but that doesn't mean a teen didn't do this. People travel with their family and occasionally, college-age students lie about their age. "Then you won't have to repair anything?" I have no idea what a gasket seal does but it sounds important and I don't need a repeat of this experience.

"I'll replace the seal and you'll be good as new." He motions to the water. "Scott coming?"

"Yeah. He's bringing fans too."

"Hope you don't end up needing to replace the tiles."

My stomach tenses.

Lord God, please no. Let the fans do their work.

Tiles are supposed to be sturdy, but I do know from past experience they can get loosened from water damage and grow mold in the subfloor below.

I groan.

Lewis stands and tugs his jeans up higher.

Fortunately for all of Anchor Cove, he does not meet the plumber stereotypes. He's trim in the waist, and his pants never reveal anything unseemly. Lewis pushes his blond hair back, and his blue eyes take on a solemn hue. "It'll be all right, Simone."

"I hope so," I grouse.

He leaves the kitchen to grab a part. I let out a long sigh then pull out my cell to text Taj.

There's a huge mess at the Sunlight Harbor property. Could you start dinner for us?

TAJ

Sure thing. When do you think you'll be home?

I glance at my watch.

An hour?

TAJ

See you then.

"Whoa, you weren't kidding about a flood."

I startle, looking up from my phone.

Scott stands there, shock on his face. "What happened?"

I explain what Lewis told me and Scott shakes his head.

"I'm sorry, Simone. I'll get working on this. You can go on home."

"Shouldn't I lock up after you?"

"You still have the pin code activated from the last tenants?"

I nod.

"Then no. I'll just shut the door behind me when I leave. Go rest. You can't do anything until we see how the floors look after this water is dried up."

I hate waiting, but I understand. "Thanks for coming out so fast, Scott."

"Anytime."

I trudge through the water and out the front door. What

am I supposed to do now? How can I just continue going on as if something momentous hasn't happened? What if Scott isn't capable of drying out the tile before damage sets in? What if mold comes in and I need to redo the entire foundation? Is that a realistic expectation or is my brain merely catastrophizing the situation?

The door shuts behind me, and I stomp down the stairs.

Breathe, Simone. God's got this.

If there's one thing I've learned over the years it's that, every time I'm convinced there's no way, God shows me a path I never imagined. I just have to hold on to past hope to get me forward. Hopefully dinner with Taj will cheer me up.

Please Lord. Please provide a way. Please let the rental dry with no other issues cropping up.

I haven't always owned multiple properties. When I arrived in Anchor Cove almost sixteen years ago, I'd been pregnant and afraid. My parents had kicked me out of the house and refused further contact. Fortunately, my grandma owned a rental here that she allowed me to permanently move into. When she passed, the house was transferred to my name. Instead of paying rent, I saved as much money from my job as I could until I bought my first property and flipped it. God's been watching over me the entire time.

He'll take care of you. He always does.

My heart rate slowly lowers as my body calms under every memory of God's care for me. He's always held me in the palm of His hands, and this flood is no surprise to Him. I'll just have to repeat this over and over until Scott has more news.

When I walk into the house, smells of fried chicken fill the air. This past school year, Taj took a culinary class as an elective and I've been living my best life ever since. Having someone else share the burden of feeding us is something I've needed. Taj often decides our meals for the week and volunteers to cook at least three of the days.

I'm thankful, when something pops up that I didn't plan for, he's able to pick up the baton and cook.

"Smells good." I peer over his shoulder.

He hums a thanks as his head bobs to the music playing on the Bluetooth speaker. My mind switches from the smells that tantalize me to the 80s music playing.

"Wait? Is this *your* playlist?"

Taj pauses in flipping the chicken. "Of course. You think I'm listening to your playlist? You weren't even here when I started the music. Plus, it's hooked up to my phone."

"But this is Duran Duran."

"'Invisible' is peak."

"How do you even *know* this song? This isn't your usual genre."

"Social media. This song is used in so many videos."

Of course. His answer is always social media. This kid's musical taste is more diverse than mine, and that's saying something. When the next song that comes on is a rap song from my youth, my point is proven. Still, I say nothing as we listen to Will Smith's version of "Just The Two Of Us."

This is one of the songs I've listened to repeatedly over the years. It got me through Taj's colicky stage and his terrible twos. I kiss the back of his head, since he's the same height as me now, and move to the cabinets.

Taj raps Will Smith's parts while I sing the chorus and ad libs. I set the table, dancing around the kitchen with a smile. Our lives haven't been easy, but there have been so many good moments with Taj that I'd do it all over again.

Yes, there was a lot of shame in being a teen mom, but God has taught me a lot. The people of Anchor Cove have helped me and shown me true community. Sure, there are a few people who judge, but there will always be haters. Doesn't mean I have to let them live rent-free in my head and disturb my peace.

And I won't, not when I'm so thankful for my son and the life God's given me.

Chapter Three

Derrick

A KNOCK AT THE FRONT DOOR DRAWS MY GAZE AWAY from the news. Who in the world would be knocking on my door?

I heave my tired frame off the couch. This morning, I pushed myself during my run and now every part of me aches. I'm not young anymore, but I'm also not very old either. There's this weird conundrum where kids believe I'm ancient and seniors think I'm still a baby.

I check the peephole and freeze. *Taj?* I open the door quickly. "Hey, man, you okay?"

"Uh, yeah. I mean, no." His shoulders droop. "I need your help."

"House burning down?"

"Nope. Still standing." He glances next door. "But maybe if it was, that would be better."

He'd rather suffer a burning building?

Uh-oh.

"What did you do?"

"Um . . ." Taj winces. "I might have broken my mom's favorite end table."

"Do I even want to know?"

Well, actually, you really do.

Because how does one break an end table?

"I was tossing a ball around, and it hit the table just right for it to fall over. One of the legs popped out. My mom's going to kill me," Taj groans. "I was hoping since you knew what to do with the golf cart, you might know your way around furniture."

It's a nice hope, and luckily for him, I actually do know a thing or two. Thanks to twenty years in the Air Force, countless PCSs (permanent change of station, AKA moving all over the world), and friends who always needed assistance, I have collected a wealth of information. Call me jack-of-all-trades.

"I'll take a look."

"Thank you so much."

I hold up a hand. "Slow your roll. I may not be able to fix it. Let me check first."

"Of course."

Taj crosses the lawn and up the stairs leading to his house. I'm not sure what I expected before stepping inside, but there's something about this place that immediately calms me. Perhaps the color scheme? His mom has decorated in a mixture of navy, light blue, and tan.

Taj rushes forward, pointing to the broken end table in the living room and a lamp missing the bulb. "Here it is."

"What happened to the light bulb?"

"Cleaned it up before I knocked on your door. There were shards everywhere. I'll happily replace that and get a lecture about throwing the ball in the house versus explaining how I broke her favorite table too."

"What's so special about it?" It looks like something you'd find in a thrift shop or one of those places that repurposes old furniture.

"It's a long story, but trust I'll be looking at the pearly gates if I don't get that fixed."

I pick up the leg and see it's cracked some, then I examine the spot it came loose from. What can I do to fix this? Would simple wood glue do the trick? Probably best to fix the crack before connecting it back to the table. After a moment, I study Taj. "Do y'all have clamps and wood glue?"

"Yes?"

I chuckle. "Show me what you got."

"Everything's in the garage."

We walk through the living room and down the back stairs into the basement where the garage opens to. There's a mishmash of every type and brand on a wooden table. Makes me wonder if she collected the tools over the years or they were gifted. There are little containers I rifle through and find wood glue and clamps.

I turn to Taj. "I've got good news and bad news."

"Bruh. Give me the bad." He squeezes his eyes shut.

"I need a drill, but you don't have one." Does his mom store it in her car? Or it's hiding somewhere in the house?

He opens one eye. "And the good?"

"I can fix everything if I get that."

"Bet." He grins. "I think Mr. Brenner borrowed the drill from my mom. He lives a couple of houses down."

"Why didn't you go to him for help?" If Taj already knew an able-bodied male, shouldn't I be the last person on his list?

"Mr. Brenner probably knew Moses. It didn't seem right to put him to work."

I barely hold in a laugh.

"Be right back."

"I'll wait outside."

I sit in front of the garage and look up into the sky. Gray

clouds cross the expanse and make no sign of letting the sun shine through. I've been here a week and still haven't seen the sun. Not that it really matters. The call of the ocean waves and the smell of salt air soothe me in a way mountains and greenery never could. Coming here to think, even with the gray skies is worth it. Still . . .

Suddenly the clouds shift and the sun peeks out. My mouth curves in a smile at the sight. I quickly avert my gaze but sigh as the warmth that heats my face. The houses on the street appear more inviting with the extra light. This is what makes Anchor Cove a coveted getaway.

"Who are you, and why are you outside of my house?"

I jump up, throat dry at the sight of the angry female before me.

"Uh, sorry, ma'am. I'm waiting on Taj. He needed help."

Oh, man.

"Are you his mom?"

Her brow arches as she crosses her arms. "Who wants to know?" she enunciates with irritation.

"Derrick Benjamin." I hold out my hand, hoping she understands I mean no harm.

She eyes my palm warily but then finally shakes it. "Simone." She brushes back a riot of curls, but it's no use as some stick to her face. Her dark brown skin glistens and is smooth. Truly, the prettiest shade I've ever seen before. There's a fierceness and capability to this woman that immediately grabs my attention.

"Wait. Derrick Benjamin?" Her brow crinkles. "Why does that sound familiar?"

"I'm renting the place next door." I hitch my thumb in that direction. Not sure if that little bit of extra information helps. Has Taj mentioned me before?

"Mom!" The shock in Taj's voice is evident, but his wide gaze panning between both of us is a dead giveaway.

"What did you do?" She puts her hands on her hips. "And why do you have my drill?"

I quickly take the tool from him and step back so they can have a discussion without me listening in.

"You did what?" his mom shouts.

"I'm sorry. I'm sorry. But Derrick's gonna fix it. Right?" Taj swings a panicked gaze my way.

"If that's okay with you," I add.

His mom rubs the wrinkled spot in the middle of her forehead. "Taj Samuel Avery."

"I know." Taj cringes. "I'm sorry. Just let Derrick fix it, *please*."

She studies me then nods her consent. I gesture for them to proceed before me. No need getting in trouble for walking into a house like I own the place. I don't want any trouble.

Way to stay under the radar.

Part of me regrets letting Taj know he could reach out for help, but at the same time, the familiar drum of energy coursing through me as I handle the saw clears my mind in the way nothing else has. I'm completely focused on the task in front of me and every bit of anxiety seeps from me as I work on repairing the end table.

Maybe I really should find a part time job in Anchor Cove. If part-time work could steady my mind as easily as the little things I've done to help Taj do, it may be worth sacrificing my vacation time.

Working negates the whole point of a retreat.

But I shut the voice off and continue my repairs, happy for the quiet mind, happy for the reprieve.

Simone

Somehow one of my tenants has managed to make acquaintances with my son and now he's in my house. I. Am. Fuming. Which is exactly why Taj keeps throwing me puppy dog eyes every chance he gets. How I let him convince me to let a renter—a *strange* man—into our home is one thing. Why I now have to thank said renter is entirely another issue.

But since Mr. Benjamin has saved my heirloom, the one thing I managed to remove from my folks' place before they kicked me out of the house, I'll hold my ire for Taj until after our summer neighbor leaves. I run a hand down the table leg and find no hint that it's been doctored on. Thankfully the table my grandma gifted me at my sixteenth birthday party is repaired. Though this house previously belonged to Nana, it wasn't filled with her furniture, so this truly is the only thing left of hers I own.

"I seriously appreciate this."

"It was no problem." Derrick runs a hand over the trim black beard covering the majority of his face. His brown skin —a shade or two lighter than mine—holds a warm tint. The weariness in his dark eyes and a line permanently etched into his forehead hint at his age.

He's got to be late thirties, right? Yet I don't spy a speck of gray hair anywhere. "How can I repay you?"

"No, don't. Please." He shakes his head. "I'm just glad I could help."

I blink, then stare at Taj, silently commanding him to thank our neighbor.

"Thanks, Derrick."

I arch a brow.

"*Mr.* Benjamin," Taj corrects. He smirks, trying to act all cute.

"Don't." I stop him. I'm *not* in the mood for his charm. "I haven't forgotten you're in trouble."

"But I solved my problem. I didn't depend on you to fix my problem," he protests.

"No, you got someone else to do your dirty work."

"I appreciate the assist, Mr. Benjamin. And I'm sorry for making you do my dirty work." Taj shakes Derrick's hand then bumps fists in a man ritual that appears to be instinctive.

My son carefully makes his way to his room. I spin around, facing the stranger who I'm now realizing is also my tenant who moved in next door for the summer.

Does he know I'm the landlord?

I clear my throat. "Thank you again. This means a lot to me." I miss Nana more than any living family member. She's the one who encouraged me and helped me return to my faith. I would've been lost without her guidance and, most importantly, her love.

"Anytime." He pauses. "Uh, I'll leave now. But don't be too hard on Taj. It's hard for young men to contain all of their energy."

"Don't I know it. He's been ripping and running since he was born."

Derrick grins, and the move transforms his face from full solemnness to genuine joy. "I get it. I go running every morning for a reason."

"So, you're telling me he won't grow out of it?"

A deep chuckle falls from Derrick's lips. "Who knows? Just be thankful he's not addicted to video games like most teens his age."

"Oh, he's all about his cell phone, but you're right." We don't own a gaming console. Never have and never saw the need for one.

My tenant ambles toward the front of the house, sliding his hands into his pockets. "See you around, Simone."

"See ya."

When he turns his back to me, I stifle a gasp. He's the man from The Oasis. The one God asked me to pray for. My fingernails dig into my palm, the need to call him back pressing on my chest like a weighted blanket. Is he okay? Was he suffering from a bad day when God told me to pray or is there more to it? But God didn't ask me to share anything with him, so I watch as Derrick leaves my house.

I could be wrong. Maybe he isn't the man from the hidden cafe. But my gut tells me he is. I just have no idea if meeting him is significant or not.

You've got my attention, Lord.

Because if my tenant is the mystery man, what does that mean for now? Should I continue praying for him? Granted, I usually pray over everyone who rents from me, whether it's for a weekend or a whole summer like Derrick Benjamin. But I also have never felt the nudge to do more like I had last week.

Taj bursts through the front door then freezes when he sees me standing in the living room. "So, Mom, about that—"

I hold up my hand. "No balls in the house. Isn't that the rule?"

He gulps. "Yes, ma'am."

"And what happens when you break a rule?"

"I have to deal with the consequences that come with that action." His words are clear because this is not the first time we've had this conversation.

There's something about parenting that means you daily relive similar conversations or literally the same ones ad nauseam. Taj is a fantastic kid, but he's still a kid.

"Does that mean no phone?" he asks.

I extend my hand, palm up. "No phone."

"For how long?" he whines.

I arch a brow.

"Sorry."

"For as long as I deem necessary."

"Yes, ma'am," he whispers, placing his cell in my hand. "I'll go to my room."

I nod and watch as he trudges down the hall like I just damaged *his* priceless heirloom.

Sinking onto the couch, I place my head in my palms as memories of Nana wash over me. It's been five years since she passed but I still miss her. The ache has lessened, but today a fresh tidal wave of grief hits me.

Tears fall down my face as I recall the one family member who showed me unconditional love. Who never held my mistakes up in front of me and assumed they were my total sum. She never condoned sin, and she certainly didn't judge others for making mistakes. Instead, Nana informed me that we all fall short of the glory of the Lord. Nana loved Jesus with all her heart, and I know He welcomed her with open arms.

"Oh, Nana, I wish I could hear your voice one more time," I murmur to myself.

At least I got to attend her funeral, even if my own parents pretended Taj and I didn't exist. Safe to say they don't want to reconcile anytime soon. But that doesn't matter, because I didn't go to the funeral for their sakes. I went for mine and for Taj, who knew his great-grandmother loved him and wanted the world for him.

I wipe the back of my hand across my face and blow out a breath. Now's not the time to lose it. I do a pretty good job at holding myself together. Tonight, when I lay down in my bed and the loneliness creeps in, I'll let the tears go freely until sleep claims me.

But for now, I've got more items to cross off on my to-do list.

Chapter Four

Derrick

I wipe the sweat off my forehead as I attempt to catch my breath. The ocean is particularly vocal this morning, the wind stirring the waves into a frenzy. Yesterday's events replay in my mind over and over. I can't get over how good it felt to be needed. Even though fixing that table was a minor thing, Simone's reaction assured me the help was far from trivial.

Something about yesterday seemed like a hint from God. Too bad I've never been great at figuring out clues. I like things stated plainly with all the steps laid out before me to be accomplished. Years of being in the military made me that way, or perhaps that has always been my nature. Who knows? Regardless, I need God to just speak to me in audible terms.

Please.

After a few more minutes of silence, I make my way from the boardwalk and begin jogging back home. As I near the driveway of my rental, a piercing scream rents the air. My breath catches as I swing my head in the direction of Simone's house.

I race up the steps just as her front door flings open and she throws herself into my arms.

"Oh my word, oh my word, oh my word." She wraps her arms around my neck in a tight squeeze.

"What happened?" I croak, then tap her arm, hoping she'll loosen her hold. However, she must have misread my signal because she holds on tighter.

"There's something in there." Her body trembles.

"Can't. Breathe."

"Oh." Her arms drop from my neck to my shoulders.

I drag in an inhale and ask the question I need to. "Something or someone?" I squeeze her middle, letting her know she's safe.

"Something. Some type of creature . . . a rodent, even."

An exhale whistles between my lips. A rodent I can handle. A person, I'd need God on my side. "You're afraid of mice?" I run my hand in circles across the middle of her back to soothe her.

"That must have been a mutant mouse because . . ." Her body shudders. "No, just no. Get rid of it, Derrick, please."

"Okay, okay." I pat her arm. "But you're gonna have to let me go."

She gasps in surprise and jumps backward out of my arms. I try to catch her gaze to make sure she's all right, but she avoids me. It's possible she's embarrassed she attached herself to me like a barnacle.

I hide a grin and nod toward her place. "I'll check it out. Where was the creature?"

"Kitchen," she whispers.

My gaze scans everywhere as I walk through the living room, down the short hall, and into the kitchen. No creature. The pantry door stands open—most likely where she saw the supposed rodent. I really hope her reaction was an exaggeration. Who wants to deal with a mutant rat?

I slowly push open the pantry door until I have a clear view of the insides. Nothing. My lips turn downward, scanning the shelves, looking for mouse droppings or the pest itself.

"Meow."

I freeze. There on the bottom shelf is the most bedraggled-looking kitten I've ever seen. At least, the mewl coming from it hints that it's a feline. Its matted fur makes it unrecognizable, sort of like a miniature swamp thing. No wonder Simone ran screaming from the house.

"Hey, you okay?"

The poor thing mewls again but takes a step out of the shadows of the cereal boxes it's hiding behind. When it doesn't make any hint of swiping at me, I cautiously reach forward to pick up the scruffball. I've never seen a kitten that looks this beat up but responds gently at the same time.

"You scared Simone pretty badly. I think you owe her an apology."

The feline responds as if in agreement.

"Okay, let's go then. I don't think she wants you living in her pantry." Though I'm not sure how that happened. How had it snuck in and gone unnoticed? Before I leave the room, I move boxes here and there until I finally spot a hole in the corner of the floor, opening to the ground below. Somehow the cat climbed up the stilts and into the kitchen.

"That's amazing." But Simone will most likely disagree. Still, I solved her problem once more.

Don't get a big head, Derrick. It's a cat, not a rat.

I amble out of the house to find Simone pacing back and forth, muttering to herself in the yard. Amusement fills me as she wraps her arms around herself. There's something about her that snags my attention every single time.

Whoa, don't look at your neighbor like that.

Right, I wasn't, merely making an assessment. Simone's a little cute when unnerved. An observation I'll now choose to ignore. I head down the stairs.

"All clear," I state.

She blinks, her gaze catching on the mat of fur against my chest. She points, her words tripping over themselves. "W-what is that . . . thing? Is that a rat? Why would you cuddle a rat? *Are* you cuddling a rat?" Her whole body convulses.

I chuckle. "Pretty sure it's a kitten." I hold it up for her to see.

She leaps back, waving her hands in front of her while shaking her head furiously. "Keep that away from me."

"Come on. It just needs a bath. Taj could use a playmate."

A single brow arches as her hands settle on her hips. "I don't think so. That boy can barely remember to clean up after himself let alone a . . . c-cat."

I study the fluffball. It's so dirty that I'm not actually sure what color it's supposed to be. Did someone bury it in mud? Did it escape from its own horrors? "Does Anchor Cove have a humane society?"

Her nose wrinkles. "I'm sure we do. I've just never been." She pulls out her cell, her fingers flying across the keyboard. "Okay. We do. It's on Seashore Drive, and they're open for another hour."

"I'll see what I can do about this guy then."

"Thank you."

"Yeah, no problem."

I move toward my side of the driveway.

Simone's voice stops me in my tracks. "Derrick?"

"Yeah?" I peer over my shoulder to find her shifting from foot to foot.

"By any chance do you know how to lay tile?"

I face her fully. "Actually, I do. Why?"

She comes closer. "I have this rental property that got flooded and I just found out the tiles need to be replaced. The old ones need to come up first and the subflooring may need to be redone as well."

"Has the property been properly dried?"

She nods. "I can pay you."

I don't really need the money, but Simone seems like the type who *needs* to pay a person. "We can work those details out later. I'm not too concerned about that."

She bites her lip. "Are you sure?"

"Positive." I hold up the cat. "Let me get this guy situated and then I can meet you at the property?"

"Sounds good. I'll text you the address."

I give her my cell number. "I'll see you later."

My steps are lighter as I walk away. I have a job, even if it lasts as long—or as short—as it takes me to fix her flooring. Happiness floods me and I grin.

Simone

I unlock the door to the previously flooded property.

My nose wrinkles at the smell. Though Scott assured me the house was dry, I can't help but think the place smells moldy or something equally horrendous. Scott insisted I could remove the old tile and replace it with new ones now, but perhaps I should consider a second opinion. There *has* to be mold or something and Scott is just too ill-equipped to figure that out.

And you think Derrick can?

There's something about the man that shouts steady and dependable, and right now, I desperately need that. Taj is always gone, because he takes enjoying his summer vacation seriously. Plus, I don't expect my fifteen-year-old son to act as a man of the house. That's not fair to him since I'm the reason he doesn't have a father.

I swallow, remembering how one decision, one choice altered my life forever. Not to mention the impact my decisions have had on my son. Yes, I've raised him in as stable a home as possible, but that doesn't discount the fact he's been fatherless the entire time.

Lord God, may my son always know You as a Father.

Since I rededicated my life to the Lord, I've prayed that my love and dedication to Him shows Taj that Jesus is always the answer and living for Him is all that matters.

A knock sounds on the door, and I shift to open it. Derrick dips his head in acknowledgment as I move back to allow him inside. He's a big man, probably six-two, and has to be at least a solid two hundred pounds. Though he doesn't seem to have any fat on him. He's just a really solid guy.

It doesn't really matter that I've noticed how handsome he is, because I don't date. Romantic relationships are something I don't want to navigate while surviving the single parent waters. Now that Taj is in high school, my mind keeps reminding me how alone I am. Sure, I have friends on the island, but they all have their own lives.

Don't focus on that right now.

"What's that smell?" Derrick asks.

"Right?" I throw my hands in the air, my thoughts immediately refocusing on the possibility of mold. I share my thoughts with Derrick.

"I don't know. It doesn't smell like mold to me."

"It doesn't?" Instinctively, I sniff again. "You're right. But what *is* that?" Because now that I realize it isn't from the flood, I'm all too aware that disaster might strike once again.

Will I have to hire another person and spend even more money out of my emergency fund to get some answers?

"Do you have a septic tank?" Derrick says slowly as if afraid to spook me.

But it's too late. The moment I hear "septic tank," my nose finally identifies the smell. "No, no, no!" I shout, rushing toward the nearest bathroom. Sure enough, waste is bubbling up. I gag, exiting into the hall, trying to find fresh air.

Derrick goes into the room, comes right back out, shutting the door behind him.

Hot tears prick my eyelids, and I clench my jaw to keep them from escaping. This was so not on my bingo card. After dealing with the dishwasher repair, the bill from Scott, and now however much I'll have to pay Derrick to put down new tile, the last thing I need is for something else to fail.

"What do I do?" I murmur, palms pressing against my eyes.

"First, you pause and take some deep breaths." Derrick's voice calls from in front of me, but I refuse to look at him.

I take his suggestion and inhale. It's not a pleasant smell, but the ache in the center of my chest begins to recede. I drag in another breath and another until the panic clawing at my insides settles to a tiny scratch of nails.

I drop my hands to my side and meet Derrick's gaze. "Now what?"

"Now we assess the damage and find out if it's something I can fix or if you need to call in an expert."

Lines in the middle of my forehead pop up. "Do you really know anything about plumbing? We don't have septic tanks, we get city sewage."

"Even better. It might be an issue for them to fix."

"First, the golf cart," I pause at his surprise. "Taj told me. But I digress. Then you were able to fix my end table, next with the tile, and now you can fix a . . ." my voice trails off. Is it a blocked pipe? "Whatever that is?" I point over my shoulder.

Derrick smirks. "I had a couple of different jobs in the military, not to mention I've always been willing to help a fellow airman in need. Fixing someone's house so they could save a penny happened often." He shrugs. "I truly am a jack-of-all-trades."

A thought pops into my mind, but I bat it away. As much as it appeals, it's something I'll have to pray about before opening my mouth in front of Derrick. Instead, I do as he says and see if he can handle the issue instead of me having to call Lewis or Jones, the man who oversees the city's sewage system.

I gesture for Derrick to go ahead. He enters the bathroom once again, while I wait in the hall for his verdict.

"Where's the main sewage line?"

"Outside."

We go out the front, down the stairs, and toward the front of the yard where the sewer lines run. But we don't need to go any farther. The ground is sodden and the smell is back.

Derrick sighs. "You'll need to call someone from the city. Hopefully, they can fix that."

I purse my lips. "This week keeps getting worse and worse."

"Why? What else is going on?"

"Isn't the tile and this enough?"

He tilts his head to the side. "True, but I already agreed to help with the tile."

"I'm not sure I can afford new tile, your salary, and whatever the pipe will cost." I have emergency funds, but I don't want to drain them in one fell swoop.

"Don't worry about paying me."

"Derrick . . ."

He shakes his head. "I'm going out of my mind with boredom."

"But you're on vacation."

"Where I am *literally* dying of boredom," he states dramatically.

The expression on his face makes me laugh. "It can't be that bad."

He gives me a look as if to say *it really is.*

"Is there a way we can bargain?" It's on the tip of my tongue to offer a discount on his rent, but I like the idea of him having no clue I'm his landlord. Besides, I actually need his rent money.

"Maybe." He rubs his beard in thought. "How about once a week, you feed me? Just send a homemade meal my way via Taj. It'll save me money on eating out so much."

"Wait . . . Have you been eating out every day you've been here?" Surely that's not sustainable?

"Not for *every* meal." He crosses his arms, a defensive look on his face.

But all I do is double over with laughter. After I wipe the tears from my eyes, I let out one last chuckle. "And this is exactly why I made Taj learn how to cook." I stick out my hand. "You've got a deal."

Derrick flashes a grin so pure, so wide, it almost shocks me, but it's gone before I can take a mental picture. Part of me wants to see it again, and the other part recognizes seeing Derrick any other way than my tenant is far too dangerous.

Chapter Five

Derrick

THERE'S SOMETHING MIND-NUMBING ABOUT LAYING TILE —in all the best of ways. Simone thinks I'm doing her a favor, but she's the one who saved me. Saved me from my thoughts and the what-ifs that have been plaguing my days. With this one small act, I help her and give my mind the break it really deserves. Not to mention I'll be getting a home-cooked meal out of the deal.

I wonder what she'll make.

Is she a meatloaf type of woman? Or maybe she likes to cook pasta dishes? Something tells me she doesn't do casseroles, but regardless of what she prepares, I'll be thankful she went through the trouble at all.

I place another tile down as the sound of the ocean filters through the open window. Today's been pretty hot, but the breeze and the shade from being inside has me thinking it's the perfect day. Besides, I prefer the outside air to A/C any day. Turning it off was a no-brainer. Plus, it'll probably help Simone save money in the long run.

Man, she's impressive. From what Taj has shared here and there, she's raising him all by herself. No help from her family or the father. Yet she owns her own home and a rental property. What does she do for work?

I shake my head. What I don't need is for my thoughts to turn toward her. I just got my mind to relax, no need to have it spin up over a woman. The ocean waves continue to soothe me as I work in a pattern that allows me to slip into autopilot.

A shuffling noise comes from the front, breaking me out of my routine. I pause to listen for more sounds and hear the turn of the lock.

"Hello?"

"It's me," Taj responds. He walks into the hallway, stopping before me. "Thought you might let me help."

"Does your mom know where you are?" I stare pointedly. Taj is a great kid, but it's like he's trying to figure out where he can cross the line and get away with something.

He rolls his eyes. "Of course she does. I don't go anywhere without alerting her."

"And you shouldn't. The world is dangerous."

Taj huffs. "Yes, she tells me this often."

"You don't believe her?"

"Bruh, nothing bad happens in Anchor Cove."

I hold in a sigh. "Every time someone says that in a movie, something bad happens."

"Bruh, are you superstitious?"

"More like cautious."

"You sound like my mom."

Taj is a good kid even if he's naive. If he thinks Anchor Cove is the one idyllic place in the US where crime doesn't happen, he's delusional.

"Look, your mom is right to make sure you're looked after and safe. I've seen some things in the military that would give you nightmares. I've also seen negligent parents, so be thankful for the mom you have. She's a blessing."

Still, I get where he's coming from. Most boys don't notice how awesome their parents are until life kicks them in the gut or death steals them.

"I know she's a good mom, but I'm fifteen. She could stand to chill a lot more, bro."

I raise an eyebrow. "The moment you graduate and go off to college, you'll miss her."

"You're probably right." A soft smile covers Taj's face.

"I know I am." I motion to the clear area on the floor. "Watch your step and come learn a new skill."

His grin is uninhibited as he saunters toward me. This kid wants a male role model like nobody's business. My heart goes out to him. I know how it is to know something is missing, but you're helpless to do anything about it. My mom was the best single parent a kid could ask for, but she was still single, nonetheless. I wanted a father around and envied my friends who went to sports games with theirs. They'd invite me to join here and there, but it was always me on the outside looking in. I see a lot of my younger self in Taj.

"What is it you do for fun?" I ask after showing Taj how he can help.

"Play ball with my friends, go to the beach, or go to church."

"Favorite sport?"

"Football, but Mom doesn't want me playing tackle." Taj grunts. "Says she wants a better quality of life for me. I'm not sure how being a millionaire messes with your life."

"You do know football players get injured, right? They retire in their thirties if an injury doesn't take them out before then."

"Yeah, but look at how many players don't get injured."

"No such thing. They may not break a bone, but they'll get a concussion, sprain something, tear something else."

"You played when you were young?"

Dang, am I old now? I smirk at Taj. The kid is amusing even when I'm on the receiving end of his snark. "Wide receiver."

"Why didn't you go to the NFL?"

"I wasn't good enough for that, so I joined the Air Force."

"What did you do in the military?"

"I came in as a bomb loader but that became too much on my body, so I cross-trained to be a maintainer, making sure aircraft were up to requirements."

Taj's eyes widen. "Did you retire?"

"I did after my third job change. It's highly unusual, but they let me switch to intelligence. Since the Air Force paid for my education, I got a business degree before I retired."

"What are you doing now?"

"Figuring out what's next, man." So much for a brain break.

"Have you thought about being a handyman? You seem to know how to do everything."

I nudge the kid with my elbow. "You just want me to fix up golf carts while I'm here."

Taj laughs. "I'm for real. My mom could always use help with her properties."

The way he says properties has me thinking he means more than two. Just how many does Simone own?

"Oh, speaking of my mom, she told me to ask you over for dinner. Something about her owing you."

"Huh. I thought she was gonna send me a doggy bag."

"Nope. I'll be setting the table for three tonight."

"Then I'll be there."

Taj reaches a fisted hand out to me, and I tap my own fist against his. There's something about the kid that makes me smile and want to help him in any way I can. I'm used to mentoring younger men; that was the whole latter half of my military career. But Taj is younger than the eighteen-year-olds who regularly enlist in the Air Force. He's not running from a bad life or running toward something. He's still trying to figure out his path.

I want to ask him questions about himself, yet my stay in Anchor Cove isn't permanent. Should I keep some boundaries to ensure this kid doesn't get too attached and become crushed when I leave? Not that I necessarily think I have that kind of power, but it's obvious he's starved for male attention.

Lord God, do I befriend him or maintain my distance?

A friend loves at all times, and a brother is born for adversity.

Chill bumps go up my arm as Proverbs 17:17 flashes through my mind. That's about as close an answer as I've received from God since I heard Him tell me to retire. My mouth is a cave waiting for the next unsuspecting fly, but I can't seem to snap it shut. I'm too stunned at hearing God answer this question when all the ones about what should come next have been . . . *ignored?*

"What next, Derrick?"

I blink, staring at Taj's eager face. Right. I have a kid to befriend. For the next few hours, I direct Taj until every single piece of tile is in its proper place.

Simone

You know that panic when a guest is coming over and everything that can go wrong in the kitchen does go wrong? That's the exact reason my heart beats like I just swam in the ocean against the tide. My air fryer's on the fritz, leaving me to hurry to get grease bubbling on the stove to make the french fries. I ran out of Old Bay seasoning, which means now my coleslaw tastes like a Southerner's instead of the way everything in Maryland tastes. Hopefully, Derrick won't notice since he's not from around here.

After the fries are finished, I go to my bathroom to clean my face. I pat it dry, then add a dab of makeup. Derrick will be here in ten minutes, and I want to look presentable, not like I lost both the battle and the war.

Does it matter what he thinks? You're not trying to catch his attention, just repay his kindness.

True, but I don't let anyone except for Taj see me without makeup. It's been part of my armor against the world for so long, I'm practically naked without it. After my cheeks are appropriately blushed and my eyes more luminous thanks to my trusty mascara, I throw on a sleeveless blouse and head to the kitchen. I turn off the stove vent, plate the food, and call for Taj.

"How come you tell me not to yell, but you always yell my name?" He looks at me expectantly, waiting for an answer.

"Boy, set the table."

He grins, grabbing the napkins and silverware. "I haven't seen you this nervous since the city inspector came for the Oceanside property." Taj starts placing the napkins down. "What's going on?"

"We haven't had company in forever."

Taj snorts. "Derrick isn't company. He's Derrick."

"What's the definition of company?"

Taj pulls out his cell phone and answers. "A visitor; guest."

"Exactly." Yes, I'm wearing the smuggest expression known to man, but sometimes you have to pop the teen ego lest it grow out of proportion. I'm not sure what it is about teen boys, but they wear superiority the way they don hoodies, which is to say all the time.

"Whatever. You have nothing to be nervous about unless . . ." Taj's eyes narrow, and he studies me with an intensity that has me stepping back. "Do you *like* him?"

I scoff. "As a human, yes. As anything else, I don't know him, so how can I like him?"

"Makes sense. Look how long it took you to like Misha, who's, like, the sweetest person in the world."

"Maybe I have a hard time liking Misha because *you* like her."

Taj's face flushes. "We're not talking about me."

"Don't like it when the shoe's on the other foot, huh?" I cackle.

"You know, only people who were born in the 1900s use idioms. The rest of the world is letting those sayings die the perfect silent death." He gives me a pointed stare.

"I can't with you."

I light a couple of candles in the center of the dining table then step back to survey my handiwork.

The doorbell rings, and I smile. "Just in time."

"You're neurotic, Mom."

"But you love me, so what does that say about you?"

"That God gave me no choice in the matter."

I toss an accent pillow at him on my way to the front door. When I open the door, a gasp escapes me, because Derrick holds a bouquet of wildflowers, looking impossibly charming. And I shouldn't be charmed, right?

"Hey, you're here." My smile trembles, because part of me is worried Derrick thinks this is more than it is.

"Uh, yeah. Taj said I was invited to dinner." Derrick looks unsure. He thrusts the flowers at me. "My mom told me to never show up empty-handed."

The uncertainty on his face softens my heart and the way he's still listening to his mama, even though he's a grown man, has my pulse fluttering.

"Thank you." I wave him in, noting the warmth of his tall frame as he passes by. "I figured a dinner invite was better than making a to-go box and kicking you out. You're doing so much for me and I want to thank you properly."

"I appreciate that."

"Derrick, come sit next to me." Taj points to the chair next to his at our round table.

My dining table could comfortably seat four and squeeze in six if necessary. I sit down beside my son, leaving an empty space between me and Derrick. The flowers, his warmth, it's all throwing me off.

I clear my throat. "Taj, wanna say grace?"

"Sure."

We bow our heads, and I let out a slow breath. The real test of tonight will be how the food tastes.

"Dear Lord, thank You for this amazing meal my mom cooked, and I did absolutely nothing to help with. Bless her and bless our stomachs. Amen."

I snort. "You're a mess."

"Yeah, but I'll help out tomorrow, 'kay?" He grins, showing all his teeth.

Thank goodness I don't have to pay for braces. "Thanks. Could you make breakfast?"

"Can't. Pastor David asked us to come in and help get the church set up for Sunday."

Derrick's brows rise. "You volunteer at the church? Willingly?"

Taj laughs. "It started out as a 'guided' suggestion from my mom and now it's willingly. The church pastor, Pastor David, is pretty awesome."

"That's cool, man. Keep that up. Helping others will always be worth the time and effort."

Shock tingles up my spine. I've never heard a grown man talk like that. "Has that always been your experience?"

Derrick meets my gaze. "I've always found it rewarding. Maybe it's because I spent my entire adulthood serving in the military." He shrugs. "Or it's just who I am."

"Probably a combo?" Taj suggests.

"I think you're right." Derrick smiles at Taj.

Our conversation flows as we eat. Derrick shares that he was born and raised in Virginia but hasn't lived there since joining the military.

"Will you go back?" Taj asks.

"I don't know. I'm waiting for direction from God."

"Wait, you got out of the military without knowing what to do next?"

"Taj," I warn. Why do kids always stick their feet in their mouths?

"No, it's okay. It's a valid question," Derrick says. "I actually heard God tell me to retire. Too bad He's been silent on the rest of the plan."

"Bruh. That's gotta be rough."

Agreed. I'm not sure I could follow God so blindly. Honestly, a twinge of conviction hits me square in the heart. *Don't beat yourself up. God hasn't asked that of you.* Still, I'd like to know I could be that brave, that obedient, if the Lord asked it of me. But right now, I don't think I am.

Is this why God had me pray for Derrick? "If you ever need an ear, I'm happy to listen. I know how frustrating a new beginning can be." My tone is almost . . . *shy* as I study my temporary neighbor.

"Thanks, Simone."

The rest of dinner goes smoothly, and soon the men are

up, clearing the dishes at their insistence. As Taj loads the dishwasher, I pull dessert out of the fridge.

"Don't start the dishwasher. We'll have more dishes to add."

"You made banana split pie?" Taj's eyes grow round.

"I didn't know you could make a pie out of it." Derrick eyes the dish. "That looks decadent."

"It's the best, man. Just wait." Taj is practically vibrating.

"Should we sit on the back deck?" I love our view of the ocean from the backyard.

"Yes, please."

I dish up three helpings, and we each grab a bowl and spoon before heading outside. As the ocean waves become our backdrop, I realize this is the most relaxed I've felt all week.

"Thanks for this." Derrick points to his bowl. "I didn't realize how much I needed a home-cooked meal."

"My pleasure. Thanks for all the work you did."

"Now it's my turn to say, 'my pleasure.'" Lines fan out from his eyes as an amused expression fills his face.

Derrick looks lighter than when he first walked into my home. Pleasure fills me. "Well, there's more work if you want it."

"Exactly how many properties do you own, Ms. Simone?"

I don't know why, but his question elicits goose bumps up my arm. Still, I grin as if not affected. "Enough to feed my family."

"Much respect."

We don't say anything more, and even Taj stays quiet. Instead, we all watch the waves and enjoy our dessert.

Chapter Six

Derrick

I SHUFFLE INTO THE BACK PEW AT ANCHOR COVE Community Church right as they get to the announcements portion of the service. They're nearing their annual summer potluck and have a sign-up sheet in the lobby.

Being retired military means I'm used to finding new churches every couple of years before transferring to another duty station. It also means I've visited about every denomination known to man, both stateside and overseas. But what I haven't really experienced until now is a sense of coming home. People turn and shake my hand, inviting me into their midst.

I consider myself a little on the introvert side with the capabilities to mask like an extrovert when required. Because of this, I smile and shake their hands, all the while wondering if I've landed in an alternate universe.

The worship leader asks the congregation to stand, and people immediately start clapping to the beat of the music. I scan the crowd, noting the diverse makeup and the different age groups represented. Everyone has various expressions of awe, gratitude, and joy on their faces as they sing along, following the words posted on the screen.

The song isn't one I recognize, but it doesn't matter. I'm not one to sing—*ever*—because I want to spare others around me. No one has ever described the sounds coming out of my mouth as joyful, so I mentally sing along.

After a few more songs, the pastor steps up to the podium. He appears to be around my age, or perhaps early forties.

"Welcome back, family." He smiles, staring out into the congregation. "Y'all, I'm Pastor David and I can't wait to talk to you today about waiting." He pauses until uneasy laughter filters through the room.

I look around, noting the nervousness on people's faces. Guess I'm not the only one who hates waiting.

"Oh yes, that lovely waiting period we've all been in. Whether it's waiting on potential bad news from a doctor, waiting to hear about layoffs from your work, or worse, waiting on God." He tilts his head. "Why do I say waiting on God is worse? Easy. His timetable is nowhere near ours."

"Preach!" someone from the crowd yells.

I stifle my chuckle. Part of me wants to look to the heavens. It's like this sermon was built with me in mind. Perhaps that's the exact reason Taj invited me to church before I left his house the other day. That kid's something else. His mom deserves all the props for how she's raising him. I've never met someone so conscious of others and respectful, yet he still has the ability to let his personality shine.

You don't see that every day.

"From birth, we've sought to understand time, and the bar constantly moves. When we were kids, minutes felt like hours, days felt like months. As we've matured, some of us have seen exactly how fleeting time can be. Look at me. I just graduated high school yesterday."

The crowd laughs.

"You're right, I didn't, but it sure feels that way. I remember that day as vividly as the day my daughter was born." He shakes his head. "Now she's twelve going on thirty and I don't know where the time went. But make me wait on something, someone . . ." His audible sigh fills the room.

I resist the urge to squirm. Haven't I been struggling with this exact thing? Waiting has never been my forte, and now it seems even more agonizing.

"There's a reason God has us wait, but I don't want to talk about that."

"Come on," someone shouts.

"Yeah, yeah, I know. We want to know *why*. Why does He make us wait? But this morning, I want to talk about *how* we wait." The pastor stops and stares into the crowd. "Any complainers out there? Like to throw a pity party when you have to wait? No? Just me?"

I wince as conviction hits. I haven't gone a single day without waking up and complaining about the lack of response from God.

"I want you to know that's perfectly human. It's perfectly natural. But what we shouldn't stay in is a response ruled by our flesh, not one by the submission to the Spirit. It's easy to complain. It's harder to look for the positives. It's easier to cry out 'why' to the Lord. It's harder to ask Him to grow you in the waiting."

My gut clenches. Is God trying to grow me? Do I need to mature in some way? I mean, I'm thirty-eight. I'm pretty sure I've arrived at maturity. *And that's doubtless why God needs to pull you to the side.*

My gramps used to say you were never too old to learn. And here I've been thinking I don't need to learn anymore.

I'm sorry, Lord.

I tune back in to listen to the pastor as he begins giving tips on waiting well. I pull my cell phone out of my pocket to take notes.

1. Praise Him daily
2. Ask the hard questions
3. Stay in the Word
4. Position yourself for blessings

I read the list again. It's pretty straightforward, yet interesting at the same time. The only one I've been doing is number three. I read the Bible every day, but maybe I need to take a look at how I'm doing so. Am I reading for reading's sake or for revelation from God?

Before I'm able to ponder that thought further, the worship team goes back on stage to lead the congregation in a final song. When it's over, I sidestep my way out of the row after the couple in front of me exits into the aisle.

"Derrick!"

I turn at the sound of my name and see Taj coming down the center aisle.

"You came," he rasps, as if out of breath.

"I said I would."

He grins up at me. "Some of us are going to do a pickup game of basketball. Want to join us? It's the young versus the old."

I laugh. "I'm in the old category, I presume?"

"Yep. So, will you join?"

"Yeah, I just need to go home and change first."

"Great. We'll meet out back. The church has a court."

"That's what's up."

I head out the front doors and start walking down the sidewalk toward the rental house when someone else calls my name. This time the voice is feminine, which could only mean . . .

Simone leans an arm outside the vehicle she's driving. "Want a ride?"

I don't *need* one, but something tells me to accept her offer. "Sure, but do you think you can find my address?"

"I think I can manage." She smirks.

And for the first time, I'm struck by her beauty. The arched brows, pert nose, and full lips. It's like the features finally form in such a way that my mind sees her beauty. She's still my temporary neighbor but now my brain is thinking *Simone is pretty*.

As I get in the passenger side of the vehicle, I tell my brain to shut up. I'm only here for the summer. I don't need to notice anyone when I'm searching for my next purpose.

Simone

"I'm glad you found the church okay." I mentally roll my eyes. Like anything in Anchor Cove is hard to find.

"Yeah, Taj told me where it was located."

"Oh." I sneak a glance at my tenant. "Did he invite you?"

"Yes, ma'am."

Why didn't I think to invite him to church? Somehow my son has become a one-man welcoming committee, and I missed out on the memo.

"Did you enjoy the service?" I ask.

"Yeah. Your pastor seems pretty knowledgeable and personable. Not an easy combination to achieve."

"True. The pastor before him was great with the Word

but a little standoffish. What did you think of the message?" It's a question I always ask Taj.

"You know, it's one of those messages where you wonder if the pastor knows exactly what you're going through because it's so spot-on."

I nod. "That's how I felt too. A little disconcerting, isn't it?"

"Mm-hm. But then I remind myself that God knew I'd be attending today, and He made sure I heard from Him . . ." Derrick's voice trails off.

"I'm glad God talks to us in all different kinds of ways." Though the silence is awful some days. Like when I asked God, *What next?* because Taj graduates in three years and there isn't a community college in Anchor Cove. His GPA is great, and he's always enjoyed learning, so leaving home seems like a no-brainer right now.

What will I do without my son around? I've spent the last fifteen years putting his needs before mine time after time. In the beginning, I needed to prove to the doubters—AKA my parents—that I *could* raise a child and raise him well. Now that need for approval has left, but the desire to protect Taj has only increased. How can I keep him safe when he's away for college?

The Lord will keep him safe.

"Mm. He does. How does He talk to you?" Derrick asks.

"Usually through others. Someone will text saying they felt the nudge to pray for me. Or someone says something I've been mulling over in prayer. Little things like that." I glance at him then back to the road. "You?"

"It used to be through Scripture."

"And now?" I speak quietly, sensing a shift in his mood. I pull the car into the driveway, placing it into Park before facing Derrick.

"Now I hear nothing." He rubs his beard. "I'm not sure what to think about that."

"But you did hear Him through the sermon today, right?" I want to reach out, lay a hand on him, and let him know he isn't alone. Only I don't know him like that. It would be awkward, right?

"I did, but . . ." He blows out a breath. "He's been so silent, Simone. It's driving me up the wall, you know?"

My hand reaches for his before I can form conscious thought. Warmth fills me as concern urges me to speak. "He never stays silent. Sometimes His silence is a way to get our attention to make sure that *when* He speaks—because He will—that we're ready to listen."

Derrick gazes into my eyes, and a shiver of awareness shoots up my spine. It's like he sees my fears and understands my heart. But that's ridiculous. Staring into each other's eyes can't do all that. I pull my hand back into my lap.

"Thank you. I needed to hear that. I've been so in my head about the whole thing. It's one reason I volunteered to help you with the tile. Keep my body occupied and hopefully my mind would follow."

"I'd be happy to give you more projects." But sooner or later, I should probably tell him I'm his landlord. I'm not sure why I've kept the news to myself. I just know I want to.

"What do you have next on your list?"

"Know anything about siding on a house?"

Derrick's brow rises. "I do. One of your rentals need repairing?"

"Yeah. Last month's storm wreaked havoc, and I'd like to get it fixed for curb appeal more than anything. I don't want renters claiming I catfished them with gorgeous photos only for them to pull up and see the awful siding."

"I'm your man, then." He clears his throat. "Happy to help you fix the place."

"Great. Do you want to take a look tomorrow?"

"Sure."

He grabs the door handle and I follow suit, exiting from the driver's side.

"Thanks for the ride." Derrick walks to his side of the grass, a pensive expression on his face.

"You're welcome." I search for something to say, not wanting the conversation to end. "What are you up to now?"

"Taj invited me to play ball with the guys at church."

"Oh." My son, the welcoming committee. "Have fun."

"Thanks." He waves and heads up the stairs.

Stop staring, Simone.

Right, because watching your neighbor take the stairs is odd. But for the first time since we met, something in the back of my mind niggles a warning. Is it because he's befriending Taj?

My gut immediately responds with a no. I don't think Derrick has any nefarious intentions and I've only seen green flags. But there's something here I can't quite figure out.

Save it for another day.

God will help me sort out my mood, because for some reason, I'm suddenly aware of my neighbor. The question follows me all the way inside and as I fix myself some lunch. I do my best to hear from God to see if my initial thought of *no* is correct. Is it because I noticed him as a man? A prickle of unease remains the rest of the day. And I have no idea if I should investigate the whys.

Chapter Seven

Derrick

Somehow, I've found a rhythm in Anchor Cove. I wake and do my morning exercise, ending with running in the sand to take in the views. Then, I do whatever repairs Simone needs help with. Occasionally, I'll check in with my mom or some of my friends who are still serving in the Air Force. And some days, like today, I go to my neighbor's house to eat dinner.

"Wait, wait, wait." Taj holds a hand in the air, barely holding in his laughter. "You told an officer to do the work himself?"

"Yep." There's something infectious about the kid's laughter that reminds me how carefree I used to be. "I wasn't going to let him micromanage me like he was some lord and I a mere peasant."

"Bro, I can't believe that." Taj wipes his eyes.

"Did you get in trouble?" Curiosity shines bright in Simone's dark brown eyes.

"No. Because in walked his boss who, unbeknownst to us, had been listening to our entire exchange. He took the officer aside and gave him a lesson on not antagonizing NCOs." At her blank stare, I decipher the acronym. "Non-commissioned officers. That's what they call people who are staff sergeants and higher in enlisted ranking."

"You lucked out." Taj points at me.

"Definitely. He could've written me up for talking back like that."

"Do you miss the military?" Taj asks.

This is the first question that pops into my head some mornings, and each time I have the same reply. "No. I thought I would because I gave it twenty years of my life. But now I feel . . . free." Huh. I don't think I've ever articulated that before now, but the word is apt.

"I can't imagine devoting myself to a career for twenty years then suddenly changing directions." Simone rests her chin on her hand.

"Sure, you can." I gesture toward her son. "Taj will be eighteen in a few years and then boom, you'll be an empty nester. Being a parent is almost like a career, but different since there's no retirement."

Darkness flashes in her eyes and I mentally kick myself. Obviously, she's well aware of how old Taj is. And judging by the look on her face, dreading the change already.

"Sorry. I shouldn't have said that."

"No, you're right." She forces her lips into a tight smile. "I'll miss him a lot." She rubs Taj's head.

"Mom." Taj ducks, flashing an embarrassed look my way.

"Do you know what your plan is after high school?" Taj has a firm head on his shoulders. I bet whatever he's interested in studying would take him places.

"I haven't decided. There are some things I'm considering, but . . ." He shrugs. "I'm not one hundred percent sure yet."

"Nothing wrong with that. Seek God's guidance and He'll show up." The words are automatic, but as they echo in my head, I realize how much I haven't taken my own advice.

Every single day since I retired, I've asked God for His guidance. It's time to remember He *always* shows up. Now that I'm not wearing a uniform and answering to someone else, perhaps I can find out what else I'm interested in.

"Well, there's still plenty of time left." False cheer rings in Simone's voice.

But I pick up the hint. "Plenty. You're only a sophomore." My phone rings, and I blink in surprise. "Sorry about that."

"No, take it." Taj gets up. "I'll do the dishes."

"And I'll grab dessert," Simone adds.

"Thanks." *Mom* flashes on the Caller ID and I swipe the talk button. "Hey, everything okay?"

"Well . . . I may have got into a little accident."

I swallow. "May have? How little? Where? Are you okay?"

"I'm in the ER getting checked as a precaution because my airbag deployed and the EMT advised me to."

Airbag? That doesn't sound little. "Have you seen a doctor yet?"

"Yes. I'm okay. Just some bruising on my nose and an achy back. My wrist is sprained as well."

I squeeze the bridge of my nose. "Your dominant hand?"

"No, my left."

Small miracle. "Do you need me to come? I could be there in a few hours."

"Derrick, no. I'm fine. I merely wanted to tell you so you're aware, not because I need a babysitter."

"But Mama—" She was in a car accident. I'm not trying to babysit but take care of the woman who raised me.

"Don't 'but Mama' me. I'm not so badly injured that I'm

incapable of looking after myself. If it were worse, I wouldn't stop you."

Ugh. Mom can be stubborn, but she also has a point. There isn't much more I can do for her if she's still able to do what she needs to. "Maybe *you* need a vacation to the beach."

"You do *not* want me underfoot to make you more anxious about the future."

"You won't."

She snorts. "Please, son, you've been sidestepping a conversation about your future with me since you told me you're retiring."

"Not because I don't want to hear your opinion, but because I was seeking God's first. I promise." I run my hand across the top of my head. "It's no trouble. I rented a two-bedroom, which means there's already space for you here if you want to visit. I'll pay for a car service if you don't want to get behind the wheel so soon."

"Let me think about it, okay?"

"Please do." Knowing she's been in an accident bad enough to deploy her airbags makes me want to come out of my skin. My mom is the most important person to me. I owe her everything.

"I'll let you know tomorrow."

"I'll call and check on you then."

"Love you, son."

"Love you too."

Simone sets a bowl of ice cream in front of me. "My famous piña colada ice cream."

"Wow, this looks amazing."

Her nose wrinkles. "I should've asked if you liked pineapple and coconut."

"Who doesn't?"

"This kid here." She hikes a thumb toward Taj.

"Then what kind of ice cream are you eating?" Because the color in his bowl looks the same to me.

"Banana. Pineapple is okay, but she's always adding coconut to it, so I opt for banana."

"You always make fresh dessert?" I ask Simone.

Her gaze darts away. "When I have company."

"How long do we have to know each other before I stop being company?"

"Right?" Taj cracks. "I told her the same thing. You're Derrick, not company."

I reach over to bump fists.

Simone shakes her head at our antics.

"Thanks for letting me take that phone call. My mom called to tell me she was in an accident."

"Oh, no. Is she okay?" Simone places a hand against my arm.

This is the second time she's done that, and I can't explain why the action moves me so much. I nod, trying to gather my thoughts and ignore the warmth of her touch. "She said she sprained her wrist. Plus, her airbags deployed, which means her car is likely totaled."

"Do you need to go take care of her?"

I huff. "Offered and got shot down. But I did invite her to come visit me and take a vacation. We'll see if she accepts. She's trying to give me space as I figure out my next steps."

"Space? Hmm. Do moms know how to do that?" Taj's lips twitch with barely contained laughter.

Simone wads a napkin into a ball and tosses it at his forehead.

Perfect aim.

"Derrick's a grown man. His mom gives him space all the time I'm sure, because he's *grown*." Simone arches a brow at Taj.

"But I'm not a little kid either."

"Hey, you want to be treated like a man?" she asks.

"Of course." Taj straightens in his seat, his full attention on his mom.

Only something tells me the other shoe's about to drop.

"Then get a job like one."

"Bruh," Taj grumbles.

My head falls back as unbridled laughter falls from my lips. When I pull myself together, I look at Simone. "You are simultaneously wrong for that and genius."

She gives a mock bow.

"Bro, don't take her side," Taj says.

"You gotta give her points for cleverness's sake."

"No, I don't." Taj frowns, then stuffs his mouth with a big spoonful of ice cream.

When I first came to Anchor Cove, life seemed like it would never feel right. But with each passing day, peace has begun to find its way through my unease. A big part of that is due to Simone and Taj's friendship. They make life on the little inlet interesting and have helped me rid myself of some of the anxiety.

Simone

I walk into The Crabbery and scan the restaurant for my friend. A hand waves in the air, catching my attention. Amy's at a booth for two along the side wall. I weave through the tables until I get to her.

"Hey, girl." I slide into the booth.

"Hey, Simone." Amy leans forward. "How are you? How's Taj?"

"He's good. Enjoying his summer." I place my purse next to me.

"Is he stuck playing video games all day or out of the house?"

"Definitely out of the house." I take a sip of the water already at the table. It's hot outside and I'm parched. "What about you? How are Chris and the kids?"

Though Amy and I are the same age, her two boys are only five and seven. She got married out of college and then had kids after dedicating a few years to her career.

"The boys are good. Chris took two weeks off so we could have a portion of summer together as a family. He's at home with them right now."

"Why didn't you say something? We could've gotten together another time."

She rolls her eyes. "Please. Mama needs to be around some estrogen for a little bit without little hands grabbing, little hands demanding, and little hands trying to tackle her." She pops one of the little crab balls into her mouth.

I grab one from the basket sitting in the middle of the table.

"And obviously I need to stop talking in third person."

"You're tired."

"So tired." Amy bursts into tears.

"Oh, girl." I grab some tissues out of my purse and pass them to her. "Is it that time of the month?"

Fat tears roll down her cheeks. "Worse."

Worse? What could be worse than— "Are you pregnant?" I whisper.

She nods. "Doctor told me yesterday. I'm thirteen weeks and can't stop crying."

"Is that what made you take a test?" I motion to her face, as if she can see the tears.

"No. He had me take a test when I went in complaining of indigestion. My mom said that means I'm having a girl with a head full of hair since the heartburn is already starting."

I remember hearing some of the old wives' tales when I first moved to Anchor Cove, five months pregnant—after I could no longer hide it from my folks. The women here loved on me and gave me all their guesses on what sex I was carrying.

"Are you happy?" I study my friend's face.

Amy's bottom lip trembles as she dries her eyes. "I am, just feeling a little overwhelmed. I thought with Nicky going to kindergarten this fall I'd finally have some peace for a little bit, you know? They're so high energy. What am I going to do if I have another boy, Simone?"

I reach across the table to squeeze her hand. "You'll do just fine because you have an amazing husband who supports you and a best friend who loves to babysit." Because babies. I loved having Taj, and sometimes I hate that I'm not married and can't have more. "Not to mention their grandparents will be eager to help. You've got this, Amy." My lips curve into a smile. "Don't forget there's a fifty percent chance it's a girl."

She lets out a shaky laugh. "Right. Chris tried to say the same thing."

"Then believe him. But if not, you'll be the best boy mom ever." Everyone thinks boys are so easy, but when they're eating you out of house and home or threatening to break things because they play *so* rough, it seems very far from easy. But the grass will always be greener to folks.

"Enough about me." Amy dabs her eyes then pops another crab bite into her mouth. "Tell me something new. Everything good with you and Taj?"

I tell her about the house flood and needing new tile.

"Oh my word, Simone. Why didn't you tell me sooner? I would've prayed, helped you find a contractor, whatever."

"I know. But I know you've been busy with the boys. Besides, God was looking out. I found a handyman who's been giving me a great deal on labor."

She leans forward. "A handyman? Someone we don't know?"

"Well." I sip some water. "He's my tenant. In town for the summer and bored. So he helps me out, and I feed him once a week." And I'm pretty sure I'm getting the better end of the deal. It's why he's been to our house twice this week for dinner. And if Taj continues throwing out the welcome mat, Derrick will be back more the following week.

"Is he good-looking?"

My face heats.

"Oh my word, he is!" Amy smacks the table. "How old is he? Where is he from? Will he move here after he falls in love with you, marries you, and gives you all the babies you could ever stand?"

I laugh. "Girl, calm down. It's not like that." Still an image of him pops into my mind. He has a commanding presence about him that, on initial meeting, didn't make me think classically handsome or eye-catching. Yet the more I get to know Derrick, the more I like looking at his face.

Amy's gaze narrows. "When can I meet him?"

"He was at church this past Sunday."

"Wait a minute." She holds up a finger. "The tall guy who was talking to Taj after service?"

I nod.

Amy giggles, a hand covering her mouth. "Oh girl, you are in so much trouble. He *is* good-looking."

"I mean, I like him in a 'he's nice' kind of way."

Simone, really? That's underselling your emotions a bit, don't you think?

"Does he make your heart flutter?"

I can't remember the last time my heart did that. Most likely the last time I watched a rom-com. "Why are your questions so difficult?"

"Because you're hopeless." She shakes her head. "Don't worry. Amy's here. I'll see if he's worthy of you."

I groan. "Please don't. Let's just enjoy our lunch and talk about your baby."

But the glimmer in Amy's green eyes tells me this conversation is far from over.

Chapter Eight

Derrick

I STEP ONTO THE FRONT PORCH AND LEAN AGAINST THE railing. The sun's finally out in full glory and just in time too. My mom agreed to come stay with me for a couple of days and let me watch over her as she recovers from her accident. She's still a little shaky but refused to let me drive down to get her. Instead, her friend is driving her up and will return in a couple of days to take her home.

I stare down the street, dragging in a lungful of salty air. The scent relaxes me, but at the same time my body itches to go enjoy the day. Mom will probably want to walk the boardwalk or visit some of the local shops. I'm sure she'll love it here. Everywhere I go in Anchor Cove, the people greet me with a smile and offer any needed assistance.

The sound of a car coming down the road snags my attention, and I straighten. An SUV slows then pulls into my driveway. I jog down the stairs and make it to the ground level just as Mom exits from the passenger seat.

"Derrick." She beams, holding out her arms.

My mom is the smallest woman I've ever met. Her five-foot frame is very petite, and she looks like a good wind could carry her away. I wrap my arms around her, careful not to jostle her in case she has the I-got-hit-by-a-truck body aches.

"How are you?" I ask.

"So happy to see you." She pulls back, studying me. "That beard looks good on you."

"Yeah?" I rub along my jaw, still not used to having hair there. Since I retired, I've been growing it out, happy to have facial hair just because I can. No clean-cut look like the Air Force requires.

"Definitely." She places her palm against the side of my face.

Uncomfortable with all the attention, I back away. "How about I grab your bags and we go inside?"

"Yes, but first meet Anita."

Mom introduces me to her friend, and I thank her for taking the time to bring her to the coast. As I lift Mom's suitcase, I slip Anita some gas money.

"You don't have to do this," she whispers.

"It's not about *have to,* it's a want to. Please take it. And thank you so much for driving her here."

"Happy to help."

"Nice to meet you," I say a little louder in case Mom's wondering what we're talking about, then I walk toward the front of the car. "Ready to go inside?"

"Yes. Show me the rental."

"I think you'll love it. The town too."

"It certainly looked gorgeous driving in. The water is so blue today."

"Sun came out just for you." I grin, holding the door open for her.

"I wonder if you'll ever turn that charm onto the ladies."

A bark of laughter escapes before I muffle the sound.

"Oh, Derrick. You're not still avoiding dating, are you?" She frowns, good hand on her hip.

"No. It's simply not a priority right now." I shrug. "You know that. I need to know my next steps."

"You don't have to be so singularly focused all the time. It's okay to have a little fun while waiting on God to provide the next direction. It's okay to find love in a time of uncertainty. Life is not one tick box at a time."

So she says, but I disagree. Early in my military career, I always believed I had no right asking a woman to marry me knowing I'd deploy and leave her alone. It seemed cruel, and I saw more divorces than I cared to admit. How could I ask a woman to take a chance on me now when I don't even have a real job?

Isn't helping Simone a job?

It really isn't, but at least helping is better than nothing.

"The guest bedroom is back here. Fortunately, both of these rooms are laid out like the primary, meaning you have your own bathroom. Oh, and the laundry room is downstairs, but if you need to use it, I'll carry anything down there for you."

"I doubt I'll need to do laundry before I leave."

"You never know. The sand gets everywhere." I set her suitcase on the floor. "Need anything?"

"Lunch." Mom pats her stomach. "Take me to your favorite place."

"You up for a walk?" Just because I walk all over Anchor Cove doesn't mean Mom wants to.

"How far is it?"

"Mile and a half?" I shrug. I legit have no clue.

"Let's do it."

We meander down the road. For a few minutes, we're silent. I know the quiet won't last, so I enjoy the peacefulness while I'm able to. Despite Mom's awareness that she can poke the bear with her questions, she goes for the jugular anyway.

"Have you heard from God?"

I stifle a sigh. "No, ma'am. But I *am* taking your advice and having fun. I've been to the local church. Made a friend." Taj ensured that.

"Meet anyone special?" Her voice is the complete opposite of nonchalant.

"Sure did. Yesterday, I met the pastor in a game of pick-up ball. The day before that, the local pediatrician, when I was invited to join a game of volleyball."

"Oh my goodness. I do hope you have the opportunity to raise a child who purposely dodges your questions." She shakes her head, like she's too through with me.

"Did I not answer the question?"

"You know that's not what I meant." Mom attempts to shove me with her hand but trips and wobbles toward the grass.

I grab her arm to steady her. "You know I'm like a brick."

"I don't know how I managed to give birth to such a big man."

"Well, it's not like I came out this way."

She huffs, and I let my laughter free. Getting under her skin has always been one of my favorite pastimes. Maybe that's why I became friends with Taj. He does the same thing to Simone.

"Any *lady* friends, son?"

"Sure. The woman next door has become a friend. Her and her son. They're pretty cool people. I think you'd like them." *Please don't read more to it than what it is.*

"Oh? How old is her son?"

"Fifteen."

"Is she a single mom then?" Mom looks up at me.

I nod. "She is. I don't know the full story. I don't feel like we've progressed as friends far enough for me to ask. But I know she's an amazing mother."

"Hmm."

I do *not* like the sound of that. The noise is full of speculation and quick judgment. But as long as Mom doesn't say anything more, I don't have to act defensive. I slow as The Oasis comes into view.

"Best food in Anchor Cove. Usually known only to the locals, but every now and then, we out-of-towners figure it out."

"Is that right?" Mom smirks.

"Yep." I pop my lips.

I guide Mom toward the back of the house and soon we're seated at a table for two. Sitting here with her is a lot different from my very first visit. For one, a few people who are eating recognize me now and wave hello. Second, I'm not alone.

Mom orders the crab cakes and I get a burger. By the time we finish, Mom seems to be in a better mood and assured that I'm not wasting away. I pay the check then we get up to leave. As we near the exit, Simone and Taj walk in. My steps falter. If I don't introduce them, I'll most likely offend them. If I do, my mom will start speculating again.

What do I do?

"Yo, Derrick." Taj grins. "What's up?"

"Hey, man." I pat the young man on the back and turn to my mom, decision made. "Mom, meet Taj and his mom, Simone. Guys, this is my mom, Carla Benjamin."

Simone

Derrick's mom sizes me up and I have no idea why. I paste on a smile and hold out my hand. "Nice to meet you."

"And it's nice to meet you. Derrick was saying how you two were his new friends who live right next door."

"Derrick's the best, ma'am," Taj states.

I glance at my son, happy he remembered to use his manners. I've gotten so many looks from people over the years, as if they were judging me for being a young mom as well as a single one. Making sure Taj behaved properly has been something I've always been conscious of.

"I think so too, young man."

"How are you feeling?" I ask. "Derrick said you were in an accident."

Ms. Benjamin studies her son for a moment, then meets my gaze. "I'm doing better. And the food here put me in the perfect mood."

"Their food is fantastic. Make sure Derrick takes you to Tidal Treats." It's my favorite ice cream parlor, but one I can't afford to visit every single day. Hence the reason I have my own ice cream maker to tide me over until my next visit.

"That sounds fun. But maybe tomorrow. I might be full for a little while." She chuckles.

I study the two Benjamins. Will this be Taj and me when he's a grown man? At fifteen, Taj is my same height at five feet five inches. But I have no idea how tall he'll be when he finally finishes growing. If he's anywhere near the same stature as Derrick, I might feel small like Ms. Benjamin surely does.

"Hey, man, why don't you bring your mom over for dinner tomorrow?" Taj asks.

My gut clinches at his offer. *But why?* Taj is a one-man

welcoming committee. This shouldn't shock me by now. When Ms. Benjamin's gaze lights up, I'm forced to piggyback on the invitation.

"Please. We'd love to have you." I force a smile. "But I understand if you two want time together." Didn't Derrick say she's leaving soon?

"We'd love to come." She stares up at her son. "Right?"

Derrick catches my gaze as if to ask *are you sure?* I dip my head in a subtle nod.

"Yeah. Thanks, guys," he replies.

The Benjamins say goodbye and we part ways.

I let out a breath once Taj and I are seated. "Since when did you get to be so friendly?"

Taj's brow wrinkles. "What do you mean?"

"You've been inviting Derrick to the house a lot."

"Because he's cool. I thought you liked him." He puts the menu down, studying me like a disease under a microscope.

"Of course I do. He's super nice and tells a great story." We always laugh when he eats dinner with us. But this moment seems like more.

"Then what's the problem?" Taj cocks his head to the side. "Is this because I invited his mom over?"

What's wrong with you, Simone? Your kid is being kind like you taught him and you've got beef with that? I mentally give myself a kick in the rear.

"No. I don't. There's no problem." I paste the fakest smile on my face, because even though I don't want to be irritated, I am. "I'm proud of you, Taj. You're so goodhearted and sometimes my Scrooge mentality kicks in." All true.

"Bruh. You're not a Scrooge. More like a hobbit. But don't worry, having me around will make sure you don't isolate yourself."

I laugh, as my grumpy attitude melts away. "Enough. Let's eat."

The next day, I spend the majority of my time cleaning the house. Taj takes one look at my manic scrubbing of the fridge, shakes his head, and walks right back out of the kitchen. I know that boy came in for a snack. But past experience has taught him if I'm cleaning the sealant of the fridge then I have a lot to work out in my mind.

And I do.

The conversation with Amy has been on repeat since I met up with her for lunch the other day. Couple that with Taj extending an invitation to Ms. Benjamin, and now my mind keeps singing the *Beauty and the Beast* song. *Is* there something between me and Derrick?

No way. He's just being helpful.

I remember the look on his face when he practically begged me to lay the tile then to do the other repairs. I'm merely saving him from boredom. There's nothing more to our relationship than business.

Only, my brain reminds me of how often I laugh at his stories over dinner. How he's always so eager to help do the dishes. How Taj is turning into a man before my eyes since he's been hanging out with Derrick. There's no doubt that Derrick Benjamin has been a blessing, but now he's becoming a deterrent to my peace of mind.

Yes, it's been ages since I dated. I tried here and there when Taj entered elementary school, before deciding that living for my son was the better way of doing things. I've always imagined having a romantic relationship would come after Taj graduated high school. But now I'm wondering if Amy is right. Is there something between me and Derrick, and I've simply been too oblivious to notice?

No, Derrick has never given you that longing gaze or leaned anywhere near you.

Yesterday there'd been hesitation in his gaze when he first spied us walking into The Oasis. When he introduced his mom, resignation had tugged his mouth into a frown. Surely I didn't imagine that? It was like he was worried about introducing us to his mom. Is it because he believes I'm interested in him?

I gasp in mortification and scrub the countertops faster.

Do I need to have a conversation with Derrick to make my no-dating stance clear? Making sure my son is growing up into a God-fearing man is where all my bandwidth goes. I don't have time to be interested in anyone, and I certainly wouldn't choose a man who isn't a resident of Anchor Cove. That would be absolutely foolish, and Simone Avery is not a foolish woman.

Except that one time I believed a boy and got pregnant, then had to admit the whole ordeal to my parents. But that's beside the point.

Since then, I've matured and done my best to walk through life as Jesus would have me do. Which means avoiding the foolishness relationships often bring.

Stop harping on the subject. Clear your mind.

By the time the Benjamins arrive tonight, the house will be sparkling. I already have dessert chilling in the fridge and the slow cooker going with the makings for pulled pork sandwiches. Until tonight, I'll clean and try to empty my thoughts of my neighbor.

Chapter Nine

Derrick

Picking out a shirt to go to Simone's for dinner shouldn't be this difficult. But knowing Mom is coming along has me reaching for another option to try on. The white shirt has a light blue plaid pattern and paired with my cargo shorts gives me a casual look. Mom might prefer I wear blue jeans since we'll be considered company, but no one in Anchor Cove wears jeans during the summer. This will have to be a compromise because even the staff at Anchor Cove Community Church dress casually.

I go to the living room right as Mom comes from the direction of her room, wearing a dress.

"You look nice."

"Cargo shorts, Derrick? We were invited over to someone's house. At least throw on some jeans."

Shades of growing up hearing that same phrase echoes in my head. Not gonna lie, this reminds me of some kind of childhood flashback, and I'm tempted to go change. Then I recall the whole mental conversation I already gave myself.

"Mom, no one dresses up in Anchor Cove. I've worn a T-shirt and workout shorts to Simone's house before. Believe me, this is me pulling out all the stops."

She shakes her head in disgust as I try to hide a smirk. "Pitiful."

"When in Rome." I offer my elbow to escort her. "Shall I walk you the whole ten feet next door?"

Mom snorts. "It's a longer walk than that door-to-door."

"Maybe so. But I don't want your old lady bones falling apart before we reach our destination."

"Hey, I was in an accident. I didn't do this." She holds up her bandage-wrapped wrist.

"I know. Just teasing." But I should probably tone it down.

I blame it on the nerves. Earlier when Mom met Simone and Taj, I saw that little glimmer in my mom's eyes. The one that has me suspecting she's planning Simone's and my engagement party as well as how many kids we'll have after we're married so we can live happily ever after. The woman watches too many romance movies and has an unrealistic view on love.

All too soon, I'm knocking on Simone's door and praying Mom knows to keep any insinuations that there's something here that isn't to herself. I've never once looked at Simone with romantic interest or vice versa. Not that she isn't a beautiful woman. She has the richest dark-brown skin I've ever seen. Not to mention the full lips and pretty ebony eyes. Her long, black curly hair always says "beach look" without trying too hard. What would it feel like to pull on a curl?

What the what?

Why are you thinking about your neighbor like that when you're about to have dinner at her house . . . with your mom?

I swallow as the door swings open. A breath leaks out when it's Taj standing in front of us. That means I have a few seconds to shove any attraction cataloging Simone's features in my mind had lit before actually laying eyes on her.

"My mom's in the kitchen but the table's all set."

"Does she need any help?" Mom asks, following Taj inside.

"Oh, no, ma'am. She said she'll be out in a couple of minutes. I think she's just plating everything." Taj motions for us to head into the dining room. "We can sit."

We reach the table right as Simone steps out of the kitchen, holding a giant tray.

"Hey, let me get that." I reach for the handles and inadvertently grip her hands instead.

My gaze shoots to hers, and my body freezes as her pretty eyes lock onto mine. My mouth dries as warmth heats my neck.

"I've got it," I murmur.

"Thanks," she says in the same tone.

This is weird. It *is* weird, right? But Simone lets go of the tray, averting her gaze. I place the platter in the middle of the table only to find Mom and Taj staring at us strangely. Great, did they see how odd that moment was too?

Locking gazes, holding hands, Simone and I have never had a moment like that before. It was like a charge went through the room, sucking all the viable air out. Instead of acknowledging the discomfort, I unload the dishes from the platter.

"Have a seat, everyone," Simone speaks into the quiet.

Thank You, Lord. The diversion is much needed. I go around the table and hold out the chair for my mom.

"Thanks, son."

"You taught him to pull out chairs?" Simone asks with a grin. "I need to teach Taj."

"Bruh, no one does that anymore."

"How would you know? Have you been on a date?" Simone arches a brow.

Taj's face flushes. "No, but there are all these women on TikTok and YouTube complaining about men opening doors and whatnot. No, thank you. I'll let her seat herself like the independent woman she claims to be."

"Or you can go with the niceties and *if* she has a problem, let her tell you," I interject. "Better to get yelled at for doing good than not getting a second date with someone you're actually interested in because you didn't act like a gentleman."

"Maybe," Taj draws out. "But I'm telling you, women today don't want that chivalry crap."

Simone stares at her son, daring him to continue. The standoff has me exchanging amused looks with Mom.

"Sorry." He glances at my mom then me.

It's okay, I mouth. He doesn't have to apologize for having a disagreement with Simone, because I've been privy to them before. Plus, my mom will understand. Still, I admire Simone for instilling good morals and values in Taj. He's a good kid and it's obvious that's a nod to his upbringing.

Simone really is an amazing woman.

But that doesn't mean what my mom thinks it means. It's possible to admire a woman for her parenting skills and for running a rental business. Simone owns at least five properties, which is impressive. I still need to ask her how she ended up owning multiple homes in a coastal town. That *has* to be expensive, right?

"So, Simone, Derrick mentioned you're a single mom."

My mouth dries, and I side-eye my mom. Did she really just throw me under the bus?

"I am." Simone dabs her mouth with a napkin.

"I know exactly how that is." Mom pats me on the head. "Derrick ate me out of house and home. I was amazed at how much money went back into my budget after he joined the military."

"Ouch. I thought you loved me," I joke.

"I might love money even more," Mom gives me a half smile that lets me know she's joking. She faces Simone. "How do you do it? Do you have family that helps?"

At that question, Simone stiffens. Obviously, her family is a sore spot. I discreetly lay a hand on Mom's arm, hoping she gets the message to curtail her questions.

"It's only us two. We have friends and church family who are there if we need them." She lets out a small breath. "What about you? Derrick hasn't shared about his upbringing."

Because I didn't think we were close enough to do that. Perhaps my friendship with Simone has advanced enough that we can have those heavy conversations.

You've already discussed faith. What's more personal than that?

Simone

Derrick's mom makes me wish Taj had kept his niceties to himself. Dinner is like an inquisition from an FBI agent. All that's missing is the lie detector test and the proverbial sweat dripping from my forehead. Only that little trickle of sweat going down my spine tells me my body still knows it's under the spotlight known as Ms. Benjamin.

"No, I didn't go to college." I answer. Who could afford it? Besides, life has taught me all I needed to know, and what I don't know can be found doing an internet search or looking up a how-to video on YouTube.

"That's a shame. A good education is important."

"Mom, respectfully, that's enough. You've been asking Simone all types of questions that aren't our business. *And*," Derrick clears his throat, "an education is important, but depending on what career field you're in, determines just how much and what type of education you need. I haven't seen anything that shows Simone is lacking in intelligence." He squeezes the bridge of his nose. "Please stop."

His mother purses her lips then her gaze flits to mine. Regret darkens her irises and she sighs. "I apologize."

I nod slowly. "Apology accepted." Our plates are mostly empty, and I want to be anywhere but here. "Are we ready for dessert?"

Derrick grimaces. "Maybe it would be better if we left." He stares at his mom as if to say *you know why*.

Part of me is sad to see him go. Normally, Taj and I enjoy our meals with Derrick, but I definitely won't miss his mother's presence.

"Are you sure?" Taj asks. "Mom made your favorite."

"Your favorite?" Ms. Benjamin echoes.

"Banana split pie?" Derrick asks.

I smile. "Yes. I know how much you enjoy it."

"We have to stay for your favorite, Derrick," his mom says.

A moment passes as mother and son share a wordless conversation. What I wouldn't give to be privy to their exchange. Finally, Derrick nods and agrees to a slice of pie.

"Great. Taj, if you'll clear the dinner plates."

"I'll help." Derrick stands.

"And I'll help with dessert," Ms. Benjamin offers.

My body tenses, but I force a smile. Is she extending an olive branch? It's always good to attempt forgiveness and give someone another chance. *Now put that into practice.*

"Thank you, Ms. Benjamin."

"It's the least I can do."

Definitely an olive branch then.

I pull the dish out of the fridge and point to the cabinet with the dessert plates. While she gets the plates, I take out the pie cutter from the drawer and make four slice marks into the pastry. Derrick's mom holds out each plate for me to add a slice, then helps me carry the dessert out to the dining room. As soon as we sit, Derrick dives in.

Pleasure goes through me at his enthusiasm. Derrick definitely has those bachelor vibes, and seeing him so grateful for a home-cooked meal makes me realize how much I've been missing out on. Cooking for my son is instinct at this point. Those frantic newborn days of him acting like a starving baby and me rushing to quell his cries have dulled with the constant eating over the years. Feeding Taj is a daily requirement that doesn't even make me blink twice.

Feeding Derrick is completely different.

I'm not sure how to put it into words, but my soul recognizes the differences even if my mind cannot articulate the reasons why. Every time Derrick greets the food with eagerness or supplies me with compliments, it's like I've accomplished something amazing even though I've been feeding my child and getting the occasional compliment before. Cooking a meal for Derrick has me breaking out my old recipe books and enjoying my time in the kitchen once again.

Our conversation shifts, having improved from the earlier inquisition, but my brain can't shake the new way I keep envisioning Derrick. I know he's a man. I *do* have sight. But I have never thought of him in that way until Amy made those comments. Now, I'm noticing every detail about him, even the way he holds his spoon and gives little noises of satisfaction with each bite.

Lord, what is going on with me?

I remain quiet the rest of the meal and soon find myself on

the front porch saying goodbye to the Benjamins. Before I go back inside, Derrick bends down to say something to his mom then jogs back up the steps.

"Hey. I just want to say I am *so* sorry about my mom. I have no idea what got into her and I. . ." He runs a hand through his hair. "I'm sorry, Simone."

"No, it's okay. I'm not sure I would behave much better if Taj ever dated." My face heats faster than the Human Torch's body. "Not that we're dating. I simply mean your mom wanted to make sure you're not keeping bad company."

His brown eyes twinkle. "I know what you meant. Maybe she did that because she's hoping for more. But I made sure she knows we're only friends."

"Good." Despite the word, my voice comes out flat. But why? Shouldn't the knowledge that Derrick's mom knows we're friends give me peace?

Then why are you upset?

No reason. I'll just go back inside and eat another slice of pie or grab a piece of chocolate from my stash in the fridge. That will have to settle my turbulent emotions.

"I'll see you tomorrow?" Derrick asks.

"Yeah. See ya." I wave then mentally kick myself. Before I can feel more foolish, I close the door, taking a moment to stare at it and let my thoughts run loose.

"What was that?" Taj asks.

I steady my heart then face my son. "I have no idea."

"You know his mom thinks you have a crush on her son, right?" Taj folds his arms across his chest.

"You'd think she'd realize people in their thirties are too old to have crushes."

Taj snorts. "Yeah, sure, Mom. That's why there are TikTok videos of people of all ages talking about people they like."

"But I don't *like* Derrick like that."

The skeptical look Taj throws my way is like a dart to the heart. "Taj . . ."

"Mom." He gives me another pointed look. "I get it. You haven't been in a serious relationship since what happened with my dad. Then what happened with my grandparents meant you were too busy trying to become an adult and raise me." He sighs like he's the one burdened. "I get it. But that doesn't mean that now isn't the time to start seeing someone. You and Derrick vibe in a way I've never seen before. Don't let old hurts hinder you."

He gives me a hug . . . willingly, then lets go. "I love you, Mom, and I want you to be happy."

"I love you too," I whisper.

I'm not sure if I like being schooled by my fifteen-year-old. Does *everyone* see something I don't? And if so, exactly what does that mean for me?

If I do decide to jump back into the dating waters, shouldn't I do so with a person who lives in Anchor Cove, not one passing through? I mean, Derrick's great and all, but I'm not sure I want to set my heart up for failure. I'm done making mistakes that have long-lasting repercussions.

Chapter Ten

Derrick

Ever since my mom left, the restless sensation has heightened making it so I *have* to move constantly. Which is why I'm walking down the Anchor Cove boardwalk after eating a TV dinner in my rental . . . all by myself.

Great. Now Celine Dion will be in your head.

I'd blame the earworm on my mom and her desire to play sad songs ad nauseam growing up, but the song really does fit my mood. After having dinner with Mom, Simone, and Taj, I realized how lonely my life has become. Devoting myself to the military kept me from realizing that. Someone was always throwing a party, inviting people over who lived far away from family. The men and women who wore the uniform became family.

And though I still have friends who text me and check in here and there, it's not the same. I feel . . . adrift.

I gaze out at the Atlantic, watching the rhythmic movement of the waves. Being here doesn't erase all the doubt, but it is healing something inside of me. I wish the distance between me and God didn't seem so huge. I want to be like it was at my last base when I turned in my retirement paperwork, knowing *clearly* He was in that choice. Something's gotta change.

A kid shrieks with laughter as the waves hit his ankles and he runs to his father, who immediately hoists the kid up into the air, prolonging the giggles. His wife comes to stand by them, and the man loops an arm around her and settles the kid onto his hip.

My mouth dries.

The picturesque scene flashes like a bright neon sign on the Las Vegas strip. *Family*. That's what I'm missing. My military family. My mom and extended family. Loved ones of my own. I've always thought having a family would be something I'd have in the future. But what woman wants a thirty-eight-year-old bachelor? Women probably think there's something wrong with me or that I have commitment phobia—which is actually the furthest thing from the truth. In not wanting to saddle a woman with endless deployments, I isolated myself.

The loneliness is all my fault.

I run a hand down my face as the truth hits. And for some reason, my next thought is of Simone. An awkwardness has developed between us since my mom's visit. Our conversation used to flow easily, and we could just enjoy one another's company. But now there's a tension I can't even describe. It's like my brain has suddenly discovered she's single, I'm single, and . . .

Mom's last comment to me before she left was to open my eyes and not miss the opportunity before me. I could've played dumb, but I knew she was talking about me and Simone. But I have nothing to offer her. No stability. No permanent job. Nothing.

Are you thinking the same way as you did about your deployments? Will you stay alone forever because of circumstances that can change and aren't permanent?

I mutter under my breath and walk away from the scene before me. The stores lining the boardwalk beckon to me, and I pause when the ice cream parlor comes into view. Tidal Treats sells fantastic ice cream. They have great customer service and a waffle cone that will cheer me up.

I open the door and inhale the aroma of the various churned flavors.

"Welcome to Tidal Treats," one of the teen employees calls out.

My gaze is on the menu, scanning the offerings before I know it, even though I order the same thing every time. The sound of the doorbell tinkling makes me turn around. Military habit. Yet when I see Simone's face, my thoughts obliterate. Having someone walk in when you were thinking about them moments ago is a little unnerving.

"Hey." She gives me a tentative smile.

"Hi."

She points toward the display. "Needed some ice cream?"

"Yep. You?"

"Always."

I crack a smile as some of the tension eases. "Let me buy yours. You can tell me why you need it today."

She tilts her head, studying me. Finally she nods. "I'll take a blueberry lemon in a sugar waffle bowl."

"Blueberry lemon?" That sounds like something that belongs in cake, not in a waffle bowl.

"It's the best. Have you tried it?"

"Nah. I've been getting their butter pecan. Two scoops in a waffle cone."

"Mm. That's delicious too. I went through a phase a few years back and that was my standard order."

Why does that information please me? "So now you're vibing with blueberry lemon?"

She laughs. "Something like that."

"What if we shake things up?" I ask.

"I don't know. What are you thinking?" She rubs her bare arms.

It's always a little chilly in here, and I want to offer her a jacket, only I don't have one. *Focus.*

"What if we pick each other's orders?"

Her ebony eyes light up. "You're on."

We both race to the display. I slowly walk along the enclosure, reading each flavor the parlor offers. Which one fits Simone the best? So far, every time I've had dinner at her place, she's eaten some dessert with fruit in it. Which means she really likes the flavor and if I chose a fruit-flavored ice cream, she probably won't be disappointed. But if we're shaking things up a bit as I suggested, then I need to go big and pray it's the right choice.

Simone lays a hand on me. "Let's do it this way. I'll order your dessert while you wait outside. When it's ready, I'll signal you to come in and then you order mine while I wait outside. Once you have my order ready, come find me on one of the benches. 'Kay?"

"All right. I can do that."

While I stand outside, watching for her to motion me back inside, I mentally review the flavors until I figure out the exact combination of ice cream-bowl options to go for.

Soon, I'm striding across the boardwalk to the bench Simone's sitting on. It's facing the ocean and has a perfect view, unblocked by lifeguard towers or families building sandcastles.

"Ready to trade?" she asks when I sit.

"Ready."

"One . . ."

I smile. "Two . . ."

"Three!"

We hold out our offerings, then look down at our ice cream, and laugh.

Simone

I take a bite of the ice cream in my waffle bowl. How did Derrick and I order the exact same choice? I glance at him. "I still can't believe it."

A full grin fills his face and brightens his brown eyes. "Who would've thought a salted caramel sundae in a waffle bowl would've been both our go-tos?"

"Not me." But it's so delicious.

"You happy with the choice?" Derrick asks.

I nod and turn my face up, eyes closed. The warmth of the sun heats my skin. Moments like this, I am completely relaxed and totally blissed out. Could the man beside me have anything to do with my current happiness or is it just my deep love of ice cream that has my heart fluttering in my chest?

"Why did you need ice cream?" Derrick asks.

"Actually, I don't know. It's just one of those days where I feel kind of blah." I stuff my mouth, so I don't have to say anything else for a few seconds. Honestly, I've been having more and more of these moments.

"I get that."

"What about you?" I angle to face him but still remain comfortable on the bench.

Derrick shoves a spoonful of salted caramel into his mouth and now I'm staring at his lips. I blink rapidly, trying to orient my thoughts then gaze into his eyes. Still, my insides warm.

"Remember I told you how I'm waiting to hear from God?"

"Yes."

"I'm beginning to realize that in devoting myself wholly to my career, I isolated myself unintentionally but intentionally." He grimaces. "That probably sounds ludicrous."

I let out a chuckle. "Not at all. Let me see if I'm tracking so far. You made some decisions regarding your career that you believed to be the right ones and that intention unintentionally isolated you."

"Right. And now, I'm alone." His Adam's apple bobs.

My heart squeezes at the sadness in his voice. "You can always come over to hang out with me or Taj if it gets to be too much." I'd never want him to feel lonely, not when we live a few feet away.

"I can't bother you two all the time."

"I don't mind." *I'm lonely too.* But I don't know how to say the truth out loud.

Derrick stares right into my gaze and my breath catches. There's such intensity in those depths that I almost lean forward.

"I have an idea, but I don't know if it's smart," he whispers.

Am I imagining things or has the distance between us decreased? I lick my lips, preparing . . . for *what?* I'm not sure I even want to admit it to myself.

"Simone!"

At the sound of Amy's voice squealing in the wind, I jerk back. She's farther down the boardwalk, waving a hand in the air. Her two boys are with her and they're wearing the cutest board shorts ever. One has sharks lining the bottom of his hem and the other is covered with sea turtles.

I stand up, trying to ignore the heat in my face that is *not* from the sun. "Hey." I reach out and wrap her in a hug then step back. "Hi, guys." I smile at her boys.

Billy steps forward and holds up his toy sea turtle. "Look what I got."

"Wow." I kneel down. "Where did you get that from?"

He grins, showing a gap in the front row of his teeth. "The arcade. Mom won it."

"She's great at the claw, huh?" Amy has won us countless stuffed animals from the crane games. I'm not surprised she's still using her skills for good.

"Who's this?" Amy whispers quietly.

I swallow. "Uh, Derrick, meet my best friend, Amy. Amy," I gesture toward Derrick, "meet my . . . friend, Derrick." I almost said tenant, but I still haven't told him I own his place. Keeping silent has made it become a big deal in my mind. Besides, he's much more than a tenant these days.

"Nice to meet you." He stands up, shifting his bowl to his left hand as he proffers his right.

"You too. I've heard a *lot* about you."

Can you kick your best friend in the shin when they're trying to embarrass you in front of a man? I'm pretty sure if there's a BFF handbook, that's been approved. But since her children are witnesses, I stick to narrowing my gaze at her and making a discreet motion across my neck.

She smirks and turns her full attention to Derrick. "I think it's so awesome how much you're helping Simone with all her properties. Is she offering you a discount?"

Uh . . .

"A discount? She's been cooking for me once a week."

More like three times, but I stopped counting a week ago. Now I invite him over every time I see him out and about, which come to think of it, has been happening more and more.

"Oh, I thought she would have lowered your rent since you're in one of her properties."

Derrick swings his gaze from Amy to me. Shock stares back at me.

"I'm in one of your properties?"

"Um, yeah. Sorry. I just . . ." My hands spread out on their own free will. "Didn't know how to say that. It seemed so pretentious and almost braggy. And I liked our friendship and didn't want anything to change."

I hold my breath, as he comes to terms with this new bit of information. Will he condemn me for not saying anything or understand where I'm coming from? Better if we could pretend like this never happened.

"I'm sorry," Amy said, breaking the silence. "I thought you knew."

I wave off her apology. "Don't worry."

"Well, we're gonna find a spot on the beach. Come find me later if you want." Amy eyes me sheepishly then hustles away with Billy and Jimmy.

"'Kay."

"Again, it was nice to meet you." Amy smiles at Derrick.

"Same."

As soon as she's out of hearing distance, I turn to Derrick. "I'm sorry. Can you forgive me?"

"Is there really anything to forgive? You wanted me to treat you like a normal person, not my landlord."

"Yes. That's exactly it." I nod enthusiastically at his response.

"But Simone . . ."

Uh-oh. Now the other shoe's going to drop. "Yes?" I ask tentatively.

"No more surprises."

I let out a relieved chuckle. "No more surprises."

"Just how many properties *do* you own?" He studies me, curiosity shining back and no condemnation, thank goodness.

"Ten."

His eyes widen. "You're a real estate genius."

"Hardly. But I am someone who loves this community and will do everything in my power to keep certain places from being destroyed. Turning the homes into rentals has been a great way for tourism to continue to thrive. I don't want Anchor Cove to become a town no one's ever heard of."

"Wow. You're amazing," he whispers.

And with the way he's looking at me, I *feel* amazing.

Chapter Eleven

Derrick

"Come on, Derrick, man. Please come with us."

I stare into Taj's pleading eyes.

Yesterday there was this weird connection with Simone. Not going to lie, it scared me. I told myself that Anchor Cove would be the place I relaxed and got closer to God. Hanging out with Simone and Taj has been great, but also has me wanting things I'm not sure I'm meant to have.

But with Taj turning those dark brown eyes at me, pleading for me to hang out on a boat with the two of them, I'm powerless to say no. I *should* say no, but I say . . .

"All right. I'll go."

"Yes!" Taj holds his hand out for a dap, so I bump my fist against his. "We're leaving in thirty minutes so Mom can pack some lunch."

I lean against my doorjamb. "I didn't know she owned a boat."

"She doesn't. It's Amy's. That's Mom's best friend."

"Oh, yeah. I met her when I ran into your mom at the ice cream shop."

Taj smirks. "Mom *loves* Tidal Treats."

They're amazing, so no shade from me. And now I want ice cream again. "Think your mom is packing ice cream?" I rub a hand across my stomach.

Taj laughs. "Yeah, she is. You should know that's her favorite go-to dessert by now."

He's right. I've been here almost a month and have gotten to know her eating habits pretty well.

A month? Is that right? I still feel like I have nothing to show for the time. My hope is an answer from God will lead to something tangible changing in my life. But so far, crickets.

At least I've made some friends while I've been here.

You just gotta keep everything friendly.

"Do I need to do or bring anything?"

"Nah, just come over in a half hour and be ready for fun."

"Bet."

Taj jogs down the stairs, and I close the door. I've been out on a boat before, but it's been a minute. I change into swim trunks and an old T-shirt. Half an hour later, I head over next door right as Simone and Taj exit the garage.

"Hey, glad you could join us." Simone smiles right as the sun shines into her eyes.

The angle of the light and the way her face is tipped up slightly means I get a complete view of her ebony eyes. They take on the deepest chestnut color, and my breath gets caught in my throat. She looks stunning.

Snap out of it.

"Derrick?" Taj asks.

I turn his way, trying to get the image of Simone out of my mind's eye.

"I asked if you want to sit up front." He points to the passenger seat.

"Yeah. Thanks, man." My legs wobble as I attempt to walk around the back of the car to the passenger side.

When's the last time a woman's beauty punched me straight in the gut? It sounds like a line, but I seriously can't remember when I've been so captivated.

I don't want to make this excursion weird, so I push all the thoughts to the furthest recesses of my mind. They'll be there to examine later when I'm all alone and can't make a fool of myself.

Simone connects her phone to the car and the Beach Boys start playing.

"Wow," I grin at her. "How old are you?"

She rolls her eyes, but a half smile plays across her full lips. "What person our age didn't have some older person in our lives listening to the Beach Boys? 'Surfin' U.S.A.' was in a few eighties movies, and don't forget how Uncle Jesse from *Full House* made them famous for our generation."

"Okay, but wait. You're a nineties baby, not an eighties baby. That makes a difference."

"Nah, 1900s old is 1900s old," Taj says from the backseat.

Simone huffs. "Look, sir, I won't tolerate that level of disrespect from a teen whose generation made chanting the numbers six-seven a thing."

I high-five her, and we laugh as Taj tries to make a case for his generation. Though I've never heard him use that slang, he's used more than my brain can keep up with.

We pull up to the harbor and park. Simone leads us down the row of boats until we reach the one belonging to her friend.

"Must be nice to have friends in high places." I place the cooler down and gesture for Simone to go first. Then I face Taj. "Hey, I'm going to go next so you can hoist the chest up and I'll haul it the rest of the way. Cool?"

"Yeah."

Once the food is onboard, Taj climbs up, then he and

Simone go through the motions to get us out to sea. I feel a little useless watching them.

Why do you always have to do something? The purpose of a vacation is to relax.

Military life programmed me to always be ready. Of course, we had moments of waiting, but even then, there was paperwork or some training to fill our time. And fun time was often scheduled so we could check keeping morale high off of our list.

All that to say, I'm not sure I know how to do nothing.

Which probably means that's exactly what God wants you to learn.

I rear back. A visceral reaction goes off in my body at the thought of learning how to be still. Of waiting around. Of hearing . . . silence.

But now that this idea of *rest* is what God is teaching me echoes rightly in my mind, I'm reminded that stillness and silence are actual spiritual disciplines. Not ones I've regularly practiced, at least not extensively. I'm able to quietly read my Bible in the morning. I can even sit and pray for about a half hour, though I've never gone any longer than that. However, I've never been on a silent retreat. I've never just been in a position where silence is the goal. Where *rest* is the lesson.

I run a hand down my face as it all clicks together. God wanted me to take a breather. Most likely because I spent the past twenty years with countless deployments and TDYs *not* resting. Or simply because He's preparing me for what's next. Regardless, stillness isn't a habit I've built into my life on a regular basis, and that's on me.

I get it, Lord.

I may not like it, but I finally understand.

Simone drives us out from the harbor but doesn't go so far

that we can't see the coastline. Meanwhile, Taj comes to sit by me.

"What's she doing up there?" I ask.

"Probably dropping the anchor. We're still in shallow waters so it'll reach the seabed."

Huh. You learn something new every day.

When Simone finishes, she comes to the table in the stern and starts unloading the food she packed.

"We've got Old Bay wings, potato salad, Utz crab chips, fruit salad, and some deviled eggs." She frowns, looking in the chest. "Why are there only drinks left?"

Taj smirks at me then stares in confusion at his mom. "Because we need drinks. Do you want us to be tainted by undrinkable water?"

"Boy, where are the veggies?" The lid of the chest snaps closed as Simone narrows her gaze at her son.

"No one wants veggies." He turns to me. "Back me up, Derrick."

I hold up my hands in surrender. "You do not come between a mom, her son, and proper nutrition."

We all simultaneously laugh, and Simone's irritation goes right out the window.

As I watch mother and son and recognize how often they include me, I can't help but think how right this all seems. Maybe I should consider something more while I wait on the Lord.

Simone

Is there anything better than being out on the ocean with the sun beating down on you?

Derrick and Taj are setting up fishing poles off the side of the boat. As I lay out, soaking up the sun, I'm staring discreetly through my shades. *Okay, definitely the company I'm keeping.*

Thank goodness my black sunglasses keep my gaze hidden. Because I never knew I needed to see a man joke around with my son, teach him basic skills like how to fish, or simply just sit with us.

When I first offered to cook a meal for Derrick, I figured it was the least I could do. When Taj invited him beyond our once-a-week agreement, I was a little irritated that our two-person bubble was being invaded. How wrong I was. There's something about Derrick Benjamin that makes my pulse quicken, though I've been denying the obvious for so long.

I like Derrick.

I'm not sure if it's wise to act on my feelings when he's only here until Labor Day. Then he'll ride off into the proverbial sunset, and I'd very much like my heart to remain intact when he does. But the more time we spend with him, the more I'm losing pieces of my guardrails. I'm not even sure how to keep my heart safe anymore.

"Yo, you got something." Taj points to Derrick's fishing rod, excitement making his voice higher.

Almost reminds me of the voice-cracking Taj of two years ago. I sit up to observe and laugh as Derrick attempts to reel in his catch. Taj pulls out his cell to record him and begins commentating.

"Watch as man attempts to once more subdue the animal kingdom with a . . ." He pauses for effect. "Fishing rod."

Derrick's deep chuckle floats across the air, and an unbidden smile fills my face. Before any of us can blink, a huge fish flies out of the air and flops right against Derrick.

"Woohoo! Homeboy said you may have won the war, but

you didn't win the battle," Taj crows. "Smells refreshing, doesn't it?"

Derrick holds up the fish, which is the length of his torso. "Do they make mouthwash for skin?"

"Body wash! Come on, my guy."

Even I have to laugh at that. Derrick glances my way, and although we're both wearing shades, it's like our gazes tangle. It reminds me of the other day when he insisted that I was amazing. My skin heated under his gaze, and I didn't want to look away.

Just like now.

Taj asks Derrick a question and the moment is interrupted. He gives Taj his undivided attention, speaking for the video Taj is creating, before my son pockets his cell phone. Derrick places his fish inside the cooler I brought specifically for this purpose.

"Great catch," I murmur. My voice sounds raspy to my ears.

"Yeah, but now I smell like fish." He looks down his body, his shirt clinging to him.

"Well, I didn't bring an extra shirt, but you can always take yours off to dry." I point to where the life vests are. "Just lay it out there."

"You sure?"

"The sun will get it quickly."

"Thanks."

When Derrick grabs the hem and heaves the garment up his body and over his head, I suddenly get his question of "you sure?" Because where has he been hiding those muscles? Not once did I ever get a hint that Derrick Benjamin, retired USAF Airman was holding a pack of abs for each working day. Oh. My. Stars.

Derrick clears his throat, and my gaze shoots upward to see a lopsided grin on his face. "You want to try?"

"Try what?" My brain is still stuck on the multi-pack abs.

"Fishing."

"Oh, no." I shake my head. "I have no problem eating fish, but I don't want to catch them, clean them, or anything else that involves them not arriving on my plate already cooked."

He chuckles. "You have strong opinions about that, huh?"

"Hey, you don't want to smell like them, so I'm not the only one with some preferences."

"That's not all you prefer, is it, Simone?" With a wink, Derrick saunters back over to Taj like he didn't just literally rock the boat.

Did he just . . . *flirt* with me?

Chapter Twelve

Derrick

I SWIPE MY THUMB, TURNING OFF THE ALARM AND FLOP backward onto my bed. As I stare at the ceiling, I allow myself to slowly wake up. A picture of Simone's beautiful face fills my mind, and I grin.

Yesterday on the water, I flirted. But only after the locked gaze that lasted forever. Then again, maybe I read way too much into simple eye contact. People gaze into each other's eyes all the time, right?

Sitting up, I shake my head as if I can get rid of the last vestiges of sleep so easily. I get out of the bed and make my way into the kitchen. A fresh cup of coffee awaits me, thanks to the brilliant genius who first thought of programming coffee makers. I take a slow slip, praying I won't burn my tongue. At the first hit of caffeine, a deep sigh escapes me.

This is how you wake up.

My thoughts drift back to Simone and the moment I winked at her. Dare I admit I actually want more from our relationship? But that's the opposite of smart, right?

You are more than just a job. What would one date hurt?

But I haven't been on a date in forever. I've been an

airman. An NCO. Then a senior NCO. I've been a friend, a mentor, but I don't even remember the last time a woman's called me boyfriend. I haven't been someone outside of my job for far too long. It's no wonder God wants me to experience rest and life outside of the military.

I made it my whole personality instead of just a profession.

Part of me wants to see if Simone could be more than a friend, but I don't want to drop her into my dumpster fire of uncertainty. My stomach rumbles so I peruse the fridge for eggs and the package of bacon I opened yesterday.

While eating, I look at the list of repairs Simone asked me to complete for one of her properties, anticipating new tenants next week.

My phone rings.

"Hello?" *Yikes.* I forgot to look at the caller ID.

"Derrick?"

I frown. "Taj?"

"Yeah, man, it's me."

"You all right?" His voice sounds funny. But also, what's he doing up so early? It's only eight in the morning.

"I got into an accident."

"What?" I take a breath, trying to will my heart to slow its pace. "Are you hurt?"

"No."

Did he sniffle? Is he crying?

I gentle my voice. "Are you sure you're not hurt, bud?"

"Yeah, just a little shaken. Mom's not answering her phone and the police are here, and I . . . Can you come?"

"Where are you?" I'm already throwing on my shoes, thankful the shorts and tee I slept in work for walking out the house ASAP.

"Cove Drive. By the library."

"Be right there." I have so many questions, but I'll wait until I see him before I attempt to get any answers. I don't want him to panic when I'm not there to keep him calm.

I jog down the steps and run over to Simone's place to bang on the door. Nothing. Guess she really isn't here. I don't know her schedule well enough to figure out where she could be at this time of day.

Never mind. What matters is Taj needs an adult by his side, no matter how the accident occurred.

Lord God, please let Taj be mentally and physically okay. Please let the cops be kind to him.

Wait a minute. Taj's fifteen and can't drive. How was he in a car accident? Was he driving illegally, or had he been involved in some other type of accident? My mind churns a thousand miles a minute as I drive to Cove Drive. Finally, the sign for the library appears, police lights flashing against the building behind it.

I pull into a parking space then jump out of my Jeep. "Taj?" I scan the area.

There are no cars with dents. There are a couple of people standing about, most likely trying to figure out what's going on. Still, no Taj. My gut clenches when I spot someone sitting at the back of the ambulance. I walk straight there, breaths coming in spurts.

Taj looks up, a bandage above his eye. "Derrick!" He hops off the back and drops his head against my chest like I imagined he'd do if I were his dad.

I circle my arms around him, thankful he appears fine for the most part. "You okay?" I whisper.

He shakes his head then groans.

"What happened?"

Taj steps back, eyes red. "A car came out of nowhere."

"Were you on your bike?" At his nod, my heart stops.

Immediately, my gaze is roaming the area, trying to find his bike. When I find the crumpled-up mess, my gut spasms. He could've seriously been injured. I pull him back into a hug, this time trying to blink moisture from my own eyes.

"They won't release me until an adult is here, and Mom's not answering her phone."

"Shh. It's all right. I'll be on standby until she can get here." I texted her myself before driving over. Wherever she is, I hope she has a friend around when she reads my SOS.

"What do they need from me?" I ask.

Taj breaks our hug, rubbing his face in the crook of his elbow as if to hide the fact he was crying. I'll have to let him know tears are totally fine. But first, I want to get him squared away.

"Uh, Officer Channing said he recommends I go to the hospital and get checked out. But Mom worries about money, and I've heard a ride in an ambulance is expensive, so I kind of refused to go in one. It's why I called."

I nod. "Bet. Want to go to urgent care? If your mom can't afford the bill, I'm more than happy to pay for it." I have savings and I don't mind at all if Taj is the reason I dip into the well.

After talking to the police, they dismiss us. Taj directs me to the Anchor Cove Urgent Care and soon we're sitting in the waiting room.

"Do you have any idea where your mom is?"

"I think she went out for a jog." Taj sighs, leaning his head against the wall.

"Really?" I've never seen Simone run or jog. Walking seems more her type of thing.

"I thought it was weird too. Women. They're strange creatures."

I crack a smile. "Glad you still have your humor about you."

"It's all the rizz I got, man."

I shake my head at the slang for charisma. It has to be the most ridiculous term out there, but a lot of my military friends have teens who speak the lingo, so it's not foreign to my ears, just makes me feel every year of thirty-eight.

"You don't need rizz with the right girl."

"Really? You think a woman will go out with a guy without any kind of charm?"

My head tilts back and forth, weighing his words. "You're right. You need rizz."

"Told ya."

"But don't underestimate the power of humor. Get a girl to laugh one moment and ask her out the next."

"So she can laugh *at* me?"

"She won't laugh at you. You think women would ask more guys out if they knew how much pressure fell on us?" I wait quietly for his answer.

"Nah. They can't handle the pressure any more than we can."

I chuckle. He might be right.

"Taj Avery?"

I stand and pause. "Do you want me to come with?"

"Yeah," he mumbles, shuffling from left to right.

We follow the nurse down the hall where she takes his vitals, height, and weight before leaving us to wait in an exam room. The moment the door closes behind her, my phone rings. Relief fills me as Simone's number flashes.

Simone

"Pick up, pick up, pick up," I whisper.

I've received multiple texts from Taj but now his phone is going straight to voicemail. Next, I call Derrick, who also texted me. Yes, he said everything's okay, but I need to hear that from Taj.

"Hey, Simone."

My eyes close at the sound of Derrick's voice. "Oh, thank the Lord. What's going on? Is Taj with you? Is he okay?"

"Breathe. He's with me and he's fine."

Tears spring to my eyes.

"We *are* at urgent care but as a precaution not because we believe it a necessity."

And now they're falling down my cheeks. "What happened? Tell me everything."

"How about I let Taj do that?"

Before I say *yes*, the sweetest voice speaks. "Mom?" The shakiness in his voice rends my heart in two.

"Are you okay, baby?"

"This lady hit me while I was riding my bike."

Oh my word. My hand covers my mouth as I try to trap the noise of shock. Taj doesn't have to know I'm close to giving in to the panic.

"Mom, I promise I was doing everything I was supposed to do. I wasn't in her way. The police even agreed with me."

"Oh, Taj, I'm not mad at you. I'm just sorry I wasn't there for you when you needed me."

"It's okay. I figured you had a good reason for jogging. Besides, Derrick came and he's got this. Wait a sec, the doctor's here."

There's a shuffling sound, then Derrick's voice. "I'll put you on speaker."

"Ms. Avery, it's Dr. Simmons."

"Yes, hi." I wince. What must she think of me? Sure, I'm driving to the urgent care now that I know where they are, but I'm *not* there now.

"I'm going to examine Taj with your permission, and I'll try and speak clearly as I do so."

"Yes, please."

Dr. Simmons mentions a cut above his eye that's superficial and won't require stitches. By the time I arrive, the exam is over and Taj has been ordered to take it easy. Dr. Simmons advised me to have some pain relievers on hand for the aches that are sure to come.

When I finally lay eyes on my son, the hug I give him is almost crushing. The fact that he squeezes me just as tight tells me how frightened he must have been.

He pulls away slowly, blinking back the emotion in his gaze. "Someone might see us."

I choke on a laugh, thankful he's joking still. "All right, let's go home."

Taj nods and we meander toward the exit. I look over his head at Derrick. *Thank you,* I mouth.

Of course, he mouths back. I'm not sure how I'll ever repay him, but I'm praising God he was around when Taj needed someone.

We all slow as we near my car. Taj turns to Derrick and his Adam's apple bobs as he holds out a hand for a dap. "Thanks, Derrick."

"Anytime, Taj."

As my son gets into the passenger side of my car, my gaze is on the man who looked after my one and only son. Our gaze locks then I walk straight into his open arms. Our embrace is one of comfort, but the more he rubs my back the more I have to fight for the tears to stay at bay. I manage to break hold to stare into his brown eyes once more. I need him to see my sincerity.

"I will never be able to thank you enough for being there for Taj."

Derrick tucks a curl behind my ear. "I was happy to help. Anytime you need a helping hand, call me. 'Kay?"

My throat aches and I want to fall into his arms again. When was the last time someone was there for me in any of the emergencies involving Taj? Sure, Amy has been able to commiserate now that she has kids, but for so long, I've dealt with every issue on my own. Today . . .

I'll never forget today.

I walk backwards and place a hand over my heart. "Thank you for caring for my baby."

"I know how much you love him."

I nod, because it's true. Taj has been my whole world since that stick read *pregnant*. I can't tell Derrick all the thoughts running through my mind. How I've *never* had someone show up for me *and* for Taj like he did today. How this simple act of kindness is upending every barrier around my heart. The interest that has been making pinpricks of awareness in my conscience is now full blown.

Am I ready to try a relationship and open my heart to more?

First, Taj and I will go home. I'll pamper my baby to make sure he's okay in hopes of easing the guilt for not being there. Others would tell me not to feel guilty, but that's something God will have to walk me through. Because I feel absolutely *terrible* that I wasn't there when Taj first called.

But I'd been on the beach, phone on silent, sobbing my heart out as the loneliness threatened to overtake me. I've done so much to make sure my son and I are provided for. My entire adult life has been me standing on my own two feet . .

and I'm absolutely exhausted. When I believed I couldn't do this alone anymore, God pointed the most obvious, flashing, *neon* arrow above Derrick's head.

While I was in tears, Taj was in an accident and someone else showed up. Someone else took the burden. I didn't have to bear it alone.

Lord, thank You for bringing someone to care for Taj when I couldn't.

Chapter Thirteen

Derrick

A KNOCK SOUNDS ON THE DOOR. I BLINK AT THE TIME, realizing an hour has passed since I started reading my Bible. I pull the red ribbon from the top of the book and slide it in between the pages, saving my spot in Philippians. Paul's words echo in my mind.

I know what it is to be in need, and I know what it is to have plenty. I have learned the secret of being content in any and every situation, whether well fed or hungry, whether living in plenty or in want.

His words speak directly to my current situation. They're exactly what I need to hear. Though I've read that passage many times, I'm finally connecting with the words like I never have before. No matter what's going on, no matter if God is speaking or growing me in a situation, I need to learn to be content because I have God in my life. I need to be in the now.

I twist the doorknob open, then pause. "Hey. What are you doing here so early?" Simone stands before me, holding a casserole dish, oven mitts covering her hands. And it's probably heavy. "Can I take that?"

"I've got it, but if you let me come inside, I'll set it down." She smirks.

I move aside, gesturing her inside. *Since when does she stop by in the morning?*

Whatever she cooked smells amazing, and my feet move me forward before I have a conscious thought of following her. The casserole must be a breakfast one, because I smell sausage, some kind of spice, and other notes I can't categorize.

"What did you make? And don't take this the wrong way, but why?"

She laughs. "I made you breakfast to thank you for yesterday."

The hug she gave me was more than enough thanks. My waist still remembers the imprint of her hug, my chest, the weight of her head as she sunk into the embrace. I won't forget that moment for a while, but I won't tell her that.

"You know that's not necessary, right? If our roles were reversed, you would've done the same thing."

She props a hand on her hip. "Are you negating my gratitude?"

"No." I shake my hands out in front of me. "Not at all. I just don't want you to go through all this trouble. You already feed me dinner more than our initial bargain."

Simone peers up at me through her eyelashes. "Then you don't want to have breakfast with me?"

My heart hammers in my chest. Is she . . . *flirting* with me? "Of course I want to have breakfast with you." Especially if she keeps looking at me like that.

"Then grab some plates and something to drink."

Her bossiness puts a half grin on my face. "Yes, ma'am."

Simone rolls her eyes, but the light chuckle floating between us speaks to our easy camaraderie. I pour apple juice into two glasses, remembering we have a love for the drink in common.

Soon we're sitting at the table in my kitchen and gazing into each other's eyes.

I clear my throat. "Should I pray?"

"Yes, please."

I bow my head. "Heavenly Father, thank You for keeping Taj safe. We pray that he has minimal aches and that he won't suffer any mental anguish from the accident. Please be with the driver and help them come to grips with their actions. And thank You for this amazing meal. Please bless Simone for her kindness toward me. Amen."

As soon as I finish, the sound of sniffles reaches my ears. I open my eyes to find Simone dabbing underneath hers with a napkin.

"Hey." I reach for her hand. "Talk to me."

"I'm so thankful Taj wasn't hurt." She sniffs. "But I can't even put into words what it felt like to know I didn't *have* to be there. That you were there, and you were taking care of my son. Derrick . . ." She pauses as if searching for the words. "The burden lightened because you were there with him. I trust you."

I swallow. Having her confidence isn't a small thing. Simone wasn't unfriendly when we met, but she was definitely guarded. Knowing she trusts me with her son, the most important person in her life, has my throat aching with emotion. Instead of voicing all of that, I squeeze her hand.

We say nothing for the next few minutes as we eat the breakfast hash she's prepared. It's filled with sweet potatoes, breakfast sausage, and some kind of leafy vegetable. It's absolutely delicious. Not something I'd ever make for myself but definitely something I want to eat.

"Derrick?"

"Hmm." I meet her gaze.

She glances to the side as if weighing her words.

I lean forward to listen to everything she wants to convey. "I hope you know you can talk to me. I promise I'll listen."

"I know you will. You've always jumped in when I needed help, and I appreciate that about you."

But . . . Why do I sense there's a shoe about to be dropped? Here I was thinking Simeone's feeling the exact same way about me that I'm starting to feel for her, and she's about to put me in the friend zone. I mentally brace for impact.

"Do you think that you and I . . ." She clears her throat. "Um, do you think you and I could be a thing? Because I really, *really* want to be more than friends."

My jaw drops, but I quickly shut it, lest she think I'm shocked in a bad way. I thought she was going to put an end to the light flirting we've been doing. But now she's put my hope into words, bringing the unspoken right into the open. Now that she has, I don't want to miss this opportunity.

"Simone, will you go on a date with me?"

Simone

My eyes flutter shut as joy fills me. I half wanted to kick myself for blurting my blossoming affections out loud but also wanted to congratulate myself for being brave enough to tell Derrick what I want. But waiting on his reply about killed me.

I'm grinning as the joy comes out in full force. "I would love to go out with you."

My eyes fill with proverbial hearts and I kind of want to swoon at his feet. But thirty-three-year-old women shouldn't act like adolescents when the guy they've been crushing on asks them out, right?

"Then I'll get to planning."

"It doesn't have to be anything elaborate." If sitting here like this is enough to give me heart eyes, then obviously I don't need him to pull out all the stops.

"Don't worry. It'll be a date we'll both remember."

Okay, I may need an old-fashioned fainting couch as I shiver with anticipation.

The rest of our conversation flows freely, and when it's over, I practically float to my house sans casserole dish. Derrick wanted the leftovers, so I happily left them with him. But I can't stay with my head in the clouds. I've got laundry to finish.

I'm putting the wet clothes into the dryer when Taj comes to stand in the doorway.

"Where were you?" Taj asks..

I blink at him. "At Derrick's."

His brows rise. "Why? Is everything okay?"

"Yes. I made him breakfast to thank him for yesterday. Speaking of which, how are you?"

"I'm fine."

"Not even achy?" My gaze roams over him from head to toe. He *looks* fine, but I know appearances can be deceiving.

Taj shrugs and winces. "Okay, so maybe a little achy. But I don't want to be stuck in the house bored all day."

"Play a video game on your phone or watch videos. *Relax*," I stress.

"Okay, who are you and what did you do with my *real* mom? Are you a pod person?"

"Boy, please."

Taj laughs and leans against the door. "So, Derrick . . ."

"Yes?" I put the dryer balls inside, buying time before turning to face the incoming inquisition.

"When are you going to admit you like him?" Taj has an impertinent smirk on his face.

I don't know how teens grow too big for their britches seemingly overnight, but the combination of humor makes it really hard to be stern. "Aren't I the adult? And isn't that *my* business?"

He scoffs. "If I waited for you to admit you liked him, you'd still be staring at him with hearts in your eyes like when we went fishing. Please, for all of our sakes, admit it so we can move on."

The gall! "You sound like an old man."

"And you sound like an invasive teen."

"Takes one to know one."

Taj makes a point to stare at his smart watch. "I'm waiting."

"Yes, I like him," I mumble.

"What was that?" He leans forward, cupping his ear. "Could you speak up? You know you like to mumble."

The sensation that rises up in you when your teen regurgitates words you've said to them is not a friendly sentiment. But I'll give my son points for cleverness.

"Don't you have somewhere to be? Something to do?"

"Nope." He pops his lips. "Nate is on vacation with his parents. Dan is volunteering at the aquarium. And Asher just got a job at Tidal Treats."

"Well, I'm going to the hardware store to grab paint for the house on Seashell Lane."

"Why don't you invite Derrick to go with you?"

"Grown folks' business, and I don't see any grown folks."

Taj laughs and I walk by him, trying to hold in my smile. "See you when I get back."

"Call my cell when you return, and I'll help lug the paint inside." His mouth twists into a mischievous grin. "Or are you going to get Derrick to help you?"

I wave a hand in the air, ignoring my precocious teen. But when I make it to the car, I let the laughter loose. I love that kid with a fierceness and can't believe how grown up he is now. He used to walk around the house with a blankie in one hand and a sock in the other. His favorite sock had dinosaurs printed all over. I had to buy multiple pairs just to prevent him from wearing the same ones every day.

These days I can mention the blankie or Mr. Sock and his face will redden to fantastic levels. I should've remembered that in the laundry room.

At the hardware store, the employee tells me it'll take a little bit to mix the paint, so I decide to wander down the aisles. I don't have a reno project on the horizon, but I'm thinking of buying a new place once the last one is paid off. I have another year—less if all my rentals continue to be fully booked—to pay the entire mortgage before I consider purchasing a new property and fixing it up.

Then again, if I don't acquire another property, that money could be used to save for Taj's college fund. Prices go up every year. What if I don't have enough saved for wherever he chooses? It's not like there's a local community college for him to attend. *Hmm, something to think about.*

My phone buzzes, so I pause in the aisle, pulling it from my purse. A text from Amy awaits me.

AMY

Woke up with a bad feeling and now the boys are laid up on the couch with barf buckets. I need some kind of good luck.

Well, Taj got hit by a car yesterday. Praise God he's fine. If you had sent this then, I would've said no luck here either.

AMY

Oh my word, girl, why didn't you tell me?

I was too busy having a meltdown.

AMY

Valid. He's okay, right?

Yeah. Derrick took him to urgent care until I met up with them. Dr. said he'd experience some body aches, but nothing broken and no concussion.

AMY

Do you think differently now?

It was God looking out for Taj.

AMY

Plus you got to spend time with Derrick, right?

Well . . . he did ask me out.

Amy sends a GIF of someone screaming then another of a woman fainting. I giggle and glance around to make sure no one is watching me act like a prepubescent teen in the hardware store.

AMY

When's the date?

Tonight

AMY

GIRL!! What are you going to wear?

I stare at my phone as my mind mentally goes through my wardrobe. Whoa. What *am* I going to wear?

Chapter Fourteen

Derrick

What does a guy plan for a date he asked a woman to just hours before? I scroll through Anchor Cove's tourist website searching for ideas. Taking her to play mini golf sounds fun, but I'm not sure that's something Simone would like. I click the sunset cruise link and find it's sold out for tonight. We could do dinner, but that's not unique nor is it me bringing my A game.

The phone rings and I glance at the caller ID. *Torres* flashes across the screen.

"Yo, Torres. How are ya?"

"Benjamin, my man, haven't talked to you in a minute."

"Yeah, well, last I heard you weren't even in the country."

"Just got back a few days ago. Cameron told me you got out. Why didn't you say anything?"

I rub my beard. Honestly, I'm a little ashamed of how I ended my military time. Not that I'm ashamed of my career, but not having the next steps made me hesitant to share my plans with my coworkers. Maybe that's why I didn't want to make a big deal of things.

"Yeah, I didn't have a retirement party. The shop threw a little something, but that was it."

"Why?"

I sigh, leaning back in my chair. "I'm not sure what's next."

"You okay?"

"Yeah. Life is good, I just don't like the unknown."

"You without a plan?" Torres chuckles. "I can't even imagine that."

I grin because he's not wrong. "Well, you should see me now. I'm trying to plan a first date."

"Oh, bet. Where you at?"

"Anchor Cove. A coastal town in Maryland."

"They have a boardwalk?"

"What coastal town doesn't?"

"Does it have a fair or an amusement park of some sort?"

"Yes. At the end of the boardwalk." I've seen the fair at a distance but have never gone. An amusement park doesn't hit the same when you're alone.

"There you go. Take her there, win a prize or two, and eat all the junk food you'll come to regret since we're not young anymore."

"Ha! Speak for yourself." I lean back in my chair, balancing on its two legs. "I could still pass a PT test and run laps around some of the younger guys."

"You talk a tough game, but you forget I'm coming back from deployment. There's no way you'd outrun me."

"Sure, Torres. You probably ate more donuts than a civilian cop." Torres is Security Forces, the Air Force's version of law enforcement. Though he carries a lot of equipment, and therefore a lot of weight on a daily basis, his love of donuts is well known by his friends.

"Hey, I didn't have a single one the whole time I was gone."

"How many have you had since you got back?"

The line goes silent, then we both fall out laughing.

"On the real," Torres says. "If you need a new career field, why not just settle where you are? You sound happy, man."

"And do what?"

"What are you doing now?"

I tell him how I've been helping Simone, which ends up turning our conversation into him giving more dating advice. Torres claims his tips have served him well the past ten years of married life.

His advice:

- Never stop flirting
- Communicate and learn how she communicates
- Have fun

"Appreciate the advice, man." The three tips seem easy enough, but also, the idea of entering a relationship is a little daunting. I've never been in a serious relationship before. Do I have the chops? Will I know how to be the best man Simone needs?

Right before it's time for me to pick up Simone, I dress in a button-down and pair the shirt with cargo shorts. Hopefully, Simone thinks I look good enough for our date and likes the idea of going to an amusement park.

After spritzing on some cologne and grabbing my wallet, I'm ready for my date. Halfway across the driveway it dawns on me that I don't have any flowers. Isn't that something one should bring on a first date? I stare down at my empty hands and grimace. *Is Simone even a flower fan?*

I glance at the time. There's no time for me to make a

detour. Hopefully, Simone will forgive my faux pas and let me make it up to her by winning a stuffed animal or two at the Anchor Cove Fair.

Lord, please let that make up for showing up without flowers or anything.

As I stand in front of her door, I tug at the collar of my shirt. It's been so long since I've dated and all of a sudden I feel awkward and unprepared.

Lord God, please don't let that show in my interactions with her.

Because despite the nerves, I want this. I want a chance to see what Simone and I can be. Who cares if my future is uncertain, because she makes the foundation under me appear.

I knock and a second later, Taj stands on the threshold with a serious expression on his face. It's a switch from his usual jovial greeting.

"Hey, everything okay?" I ask cautiously.

He gives me a head nod. "Wanted to talk to you about my mom." He pauses. "Where are you taking her?"

Okay, so he's going the protective route. I respect that. "My plan is to take her to the fair. I figure having fun will allow us to get to know each other better in a relaxing environment."

"When will she be home?"

Can Simone hear Taj at this moment? Would she appreciate Taj trying to give her a curfew or laugh? Regardless, I'm touched by the care he's showing.

"By midnight."

"Okay." Taj nods slowly then looks me dead in the eye. "What are your intentions with her?"

"I know Anchor Cove isn't my residence, but I'm not toying with your mom. I really like her, and I want to see our relationship grow. At a minimum, I want to maintain the respect we have for one another. But I'm trying to let God plan the details for everything else." Did any of that make sense to him? Will Taj respect the fact that I don't have all the answers but want to discover them anyway?

"Man, you know I've got mad respect for you, Derrick."

"Same for you, Taj."

He holds up a hand to stop my words. "But if you hurt my mom or make her cry, I will do everything in my power to make you suffer."

Well, now. "Noted."

Taj grins. "Hope y'all have a great time." He looks over his shoulder. "Mom! Derrick's here."

The emotional switch is so fast my head spins. How can this young man who makes me laugh ninety percent of the time make me so uncomfortable with his threat? And with just a flip of the switch he's welcoming me into the house. I almost want to know if there's some type of Hyde-Jekyll thing going on, but Simone walks into the living room and all thought flees.

Simone

The slack-jawed expression on Derrick's face is worth every agonizing minute I spent in front of my full-length mirror—which I'd be happy to throw away for its offensive ways. I'd been tempted to wear a dress, but Derrick texted me an hour ago to wear something casual. So after video chatting with Amy, I chose a light pink romper. The cinched belt at my waist gives me an hourglass shape and ups the outfit from casual to date status.

As I draw near to Derrick, I smile. For the first time, I catalogue our height differences. I'm five-five, and Derrick has enough inches where I can imagine the sweetest forehead kiss from him. Would his beard be scratchy to the touch? He barely had scruff on his face when he first arrived to Anchor Cove on Memorial Day weekend. Now that June is coming to a close, his face is covered with a full beard.

"Hey," I say softly.

"You look amazing," Derrick immediately replies.

Joy fills my heart at the simple compliment. He didn't say I was pretty, beautiful, or any of those words. But the way he said *amazing* echoes in my heart and has goose bumps dotting my arms.

"So do you," I say.

"You ready?"

I nod, but suddenly feel shy. *Why? This is Derrick.* He's been over to my house countless times. I've seen him almost every day of the week. But with one little word—*date*—my brain seems to understand the significance of this moment.

Derrick holds the car door open for me as I slide in. As soon as the door shuts, I speak into the quiet. "Lord, please let this night go well. I don't want to embarrass myself or lose the ease I have with Derrick. Help me shake the nerves. Amen," I murmur, before Derrick opens the door to the driver's side.

He studies me for a moment. "Did I mention how great you look? I think my heart jump-started when you walked into the room."

Oh my word! How wonderfully honest. There's an answering thump of my heart at his sincerity.

"I know my own did." I blink.

Wait, did I say that out loud?

Derrick emits a low chuckle. The sound soothes me, and I settle back against the seat, grateful some of the tension has released. I bask in the warmth of his presence and the fact that I'm going on a date. It's been *years*—literally years —and I hope that doesn't reflect badly on me as the night goes on.

"Where are we going?" I ask.

"To the Anchor Cove Fair."

"Really?" I love that place.

Derrick grips the steering wheel. "Is that a bad idea?"

"Not at all. I love it. I actually haven't been since Taj was in elementary school."

He flashes a grin. "Good. Everyone deserves a night of fun, especially you."

"You think you can take me in Skee-Ball? I'm a champion thrower."

"Oh, I've found a place to play that with each military move. You can't beat me."

This playful, competitive side of Derrick is as attractive as the side who lays tile, answers my son's emergency call, and asks me on a date early morning for the same day. Is this a situation where the other shoe has yet to drop and I'll find someone different on the inside? Because I've dated a man like that, had a child with a man like that. And then raised my son alone because of a man like that.

Is Derrick actually this good? This kind?

Memories of facing my parents alone, telling them I got pregnant, resurface. My ex's parents rejected me just as quickly as my own. None of them wanted anything to do with me and, subsequently, Taj. *Don't think about that right now. Have fun like Derrick suggested.*

Derrick has shown me he's different. If I don't trust that, I'll be full of angst our whole relationship. Or at least for the entire date.

The drive to the fair doesn't take long. Derrick purchases

a ride bracelet for both of us as well as a card for the arcade games from the ticket booth.

"Where to first?" Derrick stuffs his wallet into his back pocket.

Great question. I scan the area and point to the Skee-Ball machine. "You know what time it is."

"Oh, you want egg all over your face at the start of the date?" Derrick grins and pretends to pop his collar. "Bet."

I laugh at his bravado. We tap our arcade cards to the machines and the sound of the brown balls rolling down the chute has anticipation coursing through me.

I pick up one then glance at Derrick. "Loser buys the winner cotton candy."

"I'll take two please."

"With your own money."

"Wow. It's like that, Ms. Avery?" Derrick tosses his ball into the air. "Let's let the machine decide our fate."

"Go."

For the next few minutes, the sound of the balls falling into the holes and the occasional whoops and hollers from Derrick and me as we race to beat each other are all I hear. The rest of the world fades into the background.

"Wait, wait, wait." Derrick holds his arms out horizontally, blocking me from throwing my last ball.

"Are you trying to *cheat*?"

"No way." He steps away from me. "I just wanted to say, there's no way you can win." He points to his score. "I'm ahead by five thousand. You'd have to hit that or higher to tie."

I arch a brow then cross my arms. "So if I beat you, then I believe I deserve a better prize than cotton candy."

The slow grin that covers Derrick's face has a delicious shiver going up my spine. Does he realize how devastatingly handsome he looks when he grins with his whole self? I doubt it, because if so, he'd be wielding that like the best sword masters.

"How about I buy you whatever you want if you manage to win?"

I won't take advantage of the offer, but I'm thankful for it, nonetheless. "Deal." I turn, aim, and let the ball fly free. When it hits the ten thousand mark, the ball spins around the rim. My breath catches as I watch with anticipation.

Then it drops in.

I let out a whoop and jump in the air, pumping my fist. When I stop my celebration to face Derrick, his jaw has dropped and shock colors his beautiful eyes.

"Told you I couldn't be beat."

"Wait a second. I still have a shot." He holds up a ball.

"What?"

A mischievous grin curves his lips, and he pivots, facing the front. He aims straight for the ten thousand marker, but the ball bounces off the rim and falls straight into the zero-point hole. It's over. I won. I grab the tickets that shoot out of the machine, waving them in Derrick's face.

"Maybe I'll use my tickets and get *you* a gift."

He chuckles. "Besides the slice of humble pie you already served me?"

"That's a freebie."

His shoulders shake with laughter. "Where to next?" He gestures as if to say *after you*.

We walk to the air hockey table and immediately our competitive spirits are on display for a second time.

And that's how the rest of the date goes. We move from game to game, competing against one another. When we've exhausted all the arcade games, we hit the rides. Eating cotton candy on the Ferris Wheel reminds me I'm not a teen and the two don't mix. But as soon as my feet hit solid ground, I'm back to normal.

Derrick still looks a little green.

"You okay?"

"I'll be fine." He juts his chin toward the basketball game. "Want me to win you a stuffed crab?"

"Wow, you sound pretty confident." Everyone knows those games are rigged. You can spot the bent rim a mile away.

"About basketball? Definitely."

To my utter surprise, Derrick wins a stuffed crab, handing it to me with a flourish. I hug it to my chest, already so thankful for how this date is going.

By the time we're sitting back in my driveway, there's this warm cocoon of happiness surrounding me. This was a very, *very* good first date.

Derrick opens the door for me. My arms are stuffed with the crab, a bucket of popcorn, a stuffed unicorn, and an Anchor Cove hat. I look like a tourist, not a person who's lived here almost sixteen years.

"Thank you so much." I take a couple of steps backward. As much as I want a kiss from Derrick, I don't want to jump the gun.

He slides his hands into his pockets. "Can I see you tomorrow?"

"For work or pleasure?" My feet stop their backward peddle as my cheeks heat.

"I think you know."

I need a fan. "Of course you can."

Derrick leans forward and places the softest kiss on my cheek. "Goodnight, Simone."

As he walks away and up the stairs to his place, all I'm aware of is the remnant of his touch. "Goodnight, Derrick," I whisper.

Chapter Fifteen

Derrick

Simone and I have been texting all day. I love the texts, but also they're the most *distracting* thing ever since I should be finishing painting the inside of this house. Still, a pressing part of me wants to race over to her place to see her for a few minutes. I'd rather face-to-face over text any day. Maybe we could eat lunch together or even watch a movie.

And I want to take her on another date. Going to the fair yesterday went so well, I'm still riding on a high. Torres's suggestion of fun had been spot-on. Now I need a follow-up idea to keep the momentum going between us. I've been wracking my brain for inspiration while my hands have been on autopilot, swishing the paint brush like Daniel-san.

But where is this going? Are you going to stay in Anchor Cove?

My hands stutter to a stop. Earlier, I did a job search in the area and found nothing sustainable for the long haul. The last thing I'd ever want to be is a burden. Not when Simone's been running things on her own for the past sixteen years. I want to be an equal partner if our future continues looking bright. Unfortunately, my savings won't last for years, so a viable income is necessary. But what?

Lord God, what would You have me do?

The other day I read article after article on trusting God when He's silent. All assured me that I'm not alone. But I won't lie, it's as if I'm out to sea without an anchor. Isn't God supposed to never forsake me? That's what the Word said, and I have to remind myself of that repeatedly when doubts arise.

Lord, where are You? Why are You so silent?

"Hey, you okay?"

I whirl around at the sound of a beautiful voice. "Simone."

She holds up a large tote bag. "Thought you might be hungry."

"You brought me lunch?" Exactly what I'd been thinking about earlier—more time with her.

"Is that okay?"

I take the bag from her hand. "It's perfect. I was just thinking about spending time with you." A shy smile covers her beautiful lips and I have to resist the urge to kiss her.

Nice and slow. This isn't a race.

Not with Simone. I want to carve every moment into my soul, so I never forget her. Wow, that sounds a little cheesy, but I'm serious. Not having any direction right has made me all too aware of how much time I *don't* have to waste.

Enough thinking.

I motion for Simone to follow me to the side of the building that faces the ocean. "Did you bring a blanket by any chance?"

"No, but I know where there's one inside." She holds up a finger. "Be right back."

She comes back with a blanket and hands it to me. I drape

the cloth on the ground and start removing containers from the bag.

"Wow, looks like you thought of everything." I examine the clear containers. One looks like it holds dessert inside. Is that cheesecake?

"I know how much you appreciate dessert."

"It's my weakness." I pat my stomach. "One day I'll stop doing sit-ups and simply let the dessert gut rule."

Simone laughs. "You want a dad bod?"

"Hey, I once saw a man wearing a shirt that said it wasn't a dad bod, it was a father figure."

"Oh no." She covers her mouth, barely holding in her giggles. "That's so bad."

"Yet you're laughing."

"Out of pity."

Right. That's why her eyes are lit up like the night sky on the Fourth of July. Simone can't fool me. She secretly loves terrible puns as much as her son. Good thing I'm the man to supply them.

"What have you been up to today?"

"I've been looking at another property. My original plan was to purchase one as soon as I finished paying off the house on Clamshell Drive. Now, I'm wondering if I shouldn't put the mortgage money aside to add for Taj's college fund."

"Did you want to buy another property because you need the funds or because that was your plan?" I study her, fascinated. She was a kid when she had Taj, yet she's provided for the both of them all these years. The business acuity she possesses is amazing.

"It was my plan because I always like to have a cushion. However, the first year of a new property usually has a lot of ups and downs. I have to spend money to make money. But the sewer repairs and ordering that tile set me back a little."

She sighs. "Plus, I have no idea if Taj *wants* to go to college, but I don't want the lack of funds to be an issue."

"You know he could always get a school loan like everyone else."

Her nose wrinkles. "No one wants to be in that much debt."

Very true. It's one of the reasons I joined the military—a free education. "Have you checked your budget to see if you can afford not to get the house and still save for his tuition?"

"I mean, I have a savings started for him, so that's certainly doable, but . . ."

"What has you hesitating?"

Simone meets my gaze and her eyes begin to mist.

"Hey." I reach for her, brushing a lone tear away. "What's wrong?" I ask softly.

"I've never had someone to talk this over with. It's so . . . nice."

My heart thumps at the thought of her being by herself all these years. "Simone, what happened with your family?"

She sniffs and glances over at the water. "They didn't want me. They found out I got pregnant by my high school boyfriend and gave me the option of abortion or leaving." She gulps. "I told my boyfriend, who informed me he was a fan of the abortion option."

A faraway look fills her gaze. "But despite the opposition everyone gave me, I was already in love with my baby. Sure, I was terrified of becoming a mom so young. Yes, I hated that my parents were mad at me and that I'd become a statistic." She wipes a tear away. "But I loved Taj before I even knew who he would become."

"You are so brave." I'm in awe of her.

She shakes her head. "I don't feel like it. There are so many times when I think I'm screwing everything up.

Screwing Taj up." A wry smile twists her lips. "When I came to Anchor Cove, I found God. I found peace. And I've never looked back."

"Not even to contact your folks?" Surely, she's tried to reconcile before.

"They hung up as soon as they heard my voice. When I had Taj, I sent a photo to them, but it was returned back to me. Every single effort I've made over the years has been rebuffed. I've stopped trying now. Ball's in their court."

"I'm so sorry." The thought of my mom ignoring me, kicking me out, and all the things Simone has been through floors me. But Simone's adversity turned her into the woman she is today. Is she thankful for that or is there a bittersweetness to the growth?

"That's life, right? We all have something we're dealing with."

"Definitely true." I saw that time and again in the military. Every airman went through something, had some backstory that shaped how they approached their time in the service. Same with me.

Simone tilts her head. "What's your thing? What's your struggle?"

It's like she read my mind.

Simone

The way Derrick has listened to me has been more healing than I even knew I needed. Remembering the pain from when my folks cut ties with me reopened the old wounds their actions caused. But experiencing Derrick's sympathy, feeling the touch of his concern, it's as if the old hurt slowly sealed. If

I can be as much help to him as he's been to me, I'll do everything in my power to be there for him.

A thoughtful expression enters Derrick's eyes as he contemplates my questions. "Growing up, I actually had a hard time believing there was anything special about me." He shifts, slanting his body more towards me.

"Why?" I'm constantly thanking God for sending me such a good man.

"Because I didn't have a dad around." His head drops as he stares at the ground.

Suddenly, his easy friendship with Taj makes a lot more sense. "How did you overcome that?" I ask softly. "Or do you still feel that way?"

"The military helped me a lot. Not because the Air Force told me I was special." His grin turns lopsided. "They actually don't like to sprinkle praise profusely."

I smirk, imagining. I've seen some military movies and they don't seem like the flowery type.

"Before I joined the service, I needed everything to be perfect. I wanted to make sure my mom never had cause to worry about me. I saw how much being a single parent exhausted her. The worry about food in our stomachs and a roof over our head. So I made sure to be the man of the house."

My heart sinks. Has Taj felt this same burden? Part of me wants to run home and have a conversation with my son, but more than that, I want to listen to the man who's been here for me. I want to show him that he doesn't have to shoulder the load all by himself.

"When I see Taj, I see a kid who wants to connect with men, but also one who still acts like a kid." Derrick meets my gaze. "Do you know how rare that is? You've made sure he knows he's the child."

"Do you regret that your mom didn't give you that kind of childhood?"

"No." He runs a hand down his face. "She tried, but also she was busy working. I think your job is more conducive to you being around more for Taj and him being able to see you in the role as parent. Whereas my mom wasn't in the house, so I learned to cook early to remove that burden from her plate. I cleaned up around the house without her asking me."

I reach over and hold his hand, staring attentively as he lists all the ways he tried to show up for his mom while simultaneously losing a bit of his childhood.

My heart aches for what he went through, but I also see God's handiwork in turning it into something good and for Derrick's benefit. Because he can recognize the ways Taj needs another man in his life, but also see the ways I've still been able to give a childhood to my son unlike Derrick's own.

"And doing all of those things made you feel like you had worth?"

"Or that I could earn it somehow. Once I went into the military, I saw other guys who weren't raised like I was. One of them knew without a doubt that God loved him. No matter how many times he messed up in basic training, in our technical school, or at our first base. In fact, it wasn't until we were at our first base that I got up the nerve to ask him why he wasn't worried."

I lean forward. "What did he tell you?"

"God loved him no matter what." Derrick pauses, as if remembering the conversation. "It struck me then, that I wasn't convinced like he was. I'd been in church all my life, but I'd been trying to earn favor for as long as I could remember."

I want to wrap my arms around this man and hug him until every last bit of unworthiness leaves his body. I've begun to have such deep feelings for Derrick. Right now, those sentiments are manifesting in the form of protection, wanting to safeguard his emotions, and physically taking all of his hurts away. Knowing that's God's job and not mine, I simply sit with him.

"And now?"

"Now I know God would love me even if I never found another job. Even if I failed day after day. I'm His son and that's something that's unshakeable."

Father, thank You that Derrick discovered his identity lies solely in You and Your love for Him. I pray that my own son would recognize this. And even myself.

Because don't we all have days where we doubt how much God loves us?

Derrick curls an arm around my shoulders. I'm not sure how long we sit there, but suddenly the atmosphere shifts. I have no idea what's going through Derrick's head, but a lightness surrounds him.

I break the silence. "Are you all right?"

"Hmm. I will be." He squeezes my arm. "Thank you for listening and for lunch."

"You're welcome." I slowly shift away from him. "I have an appointment at the bank this afternoon, so I should probably get going. Will I see you later?"

Derrick starts loading the picnic basket. "Yeah." He pauses, tilting his head. "How about *I* cook dinner tonight?"

I arch a brow. "Really? That sounds amazing."

"Really. You and Taj come over, same time we usually meet, just at my place." He hands me the tote bag and blanket.

"We'll be there." I lean forward and press a kiss to his forehead. "Bye, Derrick."

His eyes crinkle at the edges, and I back away.

His lips had been too close, and the thought of pressing mine to his drums through me. But I'm not ready. I don't want to fall too fast. Been there, have the child as proof.

Living in Anchor Cove for so many years has shown me how quickly tourists leave the area. I want to keep my heart intact, but I fear it might already be too late. Because the affection I have for Derrick already makes my pulse erratic. If I kiss him, I might never recover.

Chapter Sixteen

Derrick

I'm never going to win any cooking awards, but I won't starve any time soon either. Living on my own for the past twenty years means I'm able to take care of myself. I prepare all my meals for the day and even know how to grill. But decades in front of the stove seems wholly inadequate when I realize just how much I want to impress Simone and Taj.

Dinner isn't meant to be any type of competition. I simply want to do something nice for Simone. Considering all of the times she's cooked for me . . . Just thinking about the breakfast casserole she surprised me with has me grinning to myself. What I love most about mealtimes with her is her and Taj's company. Knowing I'm not alone, connecting in the easy way we have from the very beginning . . . it means a lot to me. In the spirit of comfort, familiarity, and dare I say it . . . *family,* I throw together a dish that's always reminded me of growing up with my mom.

The doorbell rings and I check to make sure dinner is simmering on low. I've already cleaned up around the house so that I didn't have one more worry on my plate.

Taj crosses the threshold, a smile on his face. The cut on his eye is less visible and healing nicely. He shakes his thumb toward Simone. "We would've been here sooner if someone hadn't changed outfits repeatedly."

"Taj!"

I'm not sure if I should give into laughter or enfold Simone in a hug, because she appears mortified. Instead, I make a motion for Taj to cut it out and link my pinky with Simone's to get her attention.

"You look beautiful."

"Thank you," she replies quietly. Then gives Taj a side-eye so strong, I'm surprised the hair on his face doesn't fall straight off. This time, a chuckle falls from my lips before I can stop it.

"Don't encourage him," Simone grumbles.

I place a soft kiss on her forehead. "I won't," I whisper.

"Wow. You're gonna gang up on me now that you two are a thing, huh?" Taj is wagging his finger between us as if we're the issue and not his smart-aleck mouth.

I curl my arm around his neck and bring him close to give him a noogie, letting that be enough of an answer.

"Bruh, stop." Taj squirms, trying to get loose.

My knuckles continue rubbing across the top of his head, creating heat from the friction. "Apologize," I say in a mock menacing voice.

"Okay, okay, okay. I give."

I let go and he straightens, a contrite look on his face. "Mom, I'm sorry for outing you in front of your new bae."

"You're a brat." Simone smooshes his face.

We all laugh, and I can't help but want to take a mental snapshot of this moment. It's so normal, but also not. A month ago, I came here lost and feeling unmoored in more ways than one. I honestly believe these two found me.

"Something smells good." Simone studies me.

"Right. Dinner's ready." I grin and point for Simone to head toward the dining room. "Taj, come help me with the dishes."

"Okay."

He follows me into the kitchen, so I hand him the bread basket. There was actually one stocked in the cabinets. Simone really does think of everything when outfitting her rentals.

"Take those to the table and come back for the sweet tea, 'kay?"

"Yeah, I got your back. You don't have to impress me."

I huff. "Why not? Don't you count?"

He blinks at me then points a finger to his chest. "Wait. You care if I'm impressed by your cooking?"

Is it hot in this kitchen? I want to tug at my collar and avert my gaze, but the way Taj is studying me tells me he wants honesty, not evasive dialogue.

"Yes, I care. You've been your mom's whole world and she loves you so much. As a man who was raised by a single mom, I saw what happened when men didn't want to date my mom any longer because I existed. Because of that, when I decided to date Simone, it was with the understanding that you would always know how much you matter as well."

I pause, trying to get the rest of the words right. Taj needs to know he's important to me outside of the relationship I have with his mother. "This isn't simply because you're Simone's son, but because of who you are. We met before I met your mom. We became friends before I befriended your mom. I don't want to hurt you any more than I want to hurt her. So yeah, I care how you feel about tonight's dinner."

I stop, but before I can add anything more, Taj puts the bread basket on the counter and thumps against me in what I realize is his way of hugging. His head is resting against my chest as if he's waiting for me to embrace him first, so I do. Slowly, his arms come around me. I squeeze him tight.

I love Taj Avery, and all I want to do is be someone he can lean on, no matter where I am.

"You're an amazing young man. Don't ever forget that." My tone is low because I think he may be crying if the wetness appearing on my shirt is any indication.

He sniffs loudly, and I get my answer. "Thanks," he rasps. He lets go and rubs his sleeve over his eyes, then picks up the basket and reaches into the fridge for the pitcher of sweet tea. "I'll go set these out."

"I'm right behind you."

I take a moment to breathe deeply. I don't think I realized how badly I wanted things to work out between me and Simone until this heart-to-heart with her son.

Lord God, whatever You're doing in my life, whatever You have planned, could You let this be part of that picture?

I've had conversations with the Lord before about Simone. I never felt like He was telling me *not* to date her, so I took it as a green light. But right now, this ache in my chest has me praying that Anchor Cove is my future. I'm not sure how it'll all work out. This is a tourist town with many jobs terminating when the summer ends. To be blessed with something long-term seems like wishful thinking. But it's something I'm taking to prayer because I know the Man who makes the impossible possible.

Simone

Something happened.

When I catch Taj's attention, my son offers me a small smile. It's not patronizing. It's not even his normal smile. But there's something in it that pricks awareness in my heart and has me straightening in my seat. Then Derrick walks in behind him.

He looks a little emotional, and my gaze immediately flits between the two guys. What exactly did they talk about in the kitchen? Normally, I'd charge ahead to get answers, but something in my spirit tells me now is not the time. Still, unease swirls in my middle.

Derrick sets a pot on a towel in the center of the table.

"What did you make?" I ask, trying to cut through the strange tension.

He lifts the top. "Jambalaya. It's something my mom made for a comfort-food night. Just a little something from my past." Derrick gives a shoulder shrug. Is he nervous about sharing? Or is that a visible tell left over from his and Taj's conversation?

"Thanks, man. Your mom seemed cool when we met her." Taj sits next to me.

"Not as cool as your mom though, right?" Derrick takes the chair across from me, and for once, I'm thankful these round tables are spacious.

Why? Don't you want to be closer to Derrick?

"Definitely not, but no offense to her."

Derrick chuckles, then lifts his chin toward Taj. "You want to say grace?"

My son eyes me as if asking my permission, so I close my eyes and bow my head. They're carrying on like normal and I don't want to signal that I'm in turmoil.

Taj clears his throat. "Heavenly Father, thank You for the meal Derrick provided for us. May it bring us all closer together. Amen."

Heavenly Father, keep my tears out of sight. Because the hot liquid is dangerously close. If I open my eyes, will they flood out or should I blink rapidly and hope it fans them back into the ducts? I've never heard such a simple yet heartfelt prayer from my son's lips. I'm in awe of how he's changed over the summer. Some of that is obviously due to Derrick's impact. I'm not sure if he has any clue how much Taj looks up to him, and honestly, that kind of scares me. I don't want my son to get so attached that when—God willing, *if*—Derrick leaves, Taj is never the same.

Or do you mean you'll *never be the same?*

Regardless if it's me, Taj, or both of us, a cloak of regret falls on me. Because sitting in this house, on Derrick's turf, and watching him serve us a meal he cooked with his own two hands that represents part of his childhood . . . My heart is going *yes, let this be forever* and my mind is trying to find the emergency brake.

What have I done, dating a man who doesn't have roots in Anchor Cove?

I thought denying the attraction between us was dumb. But maybe denying the attraction kept me safe. Kept Taj safe. Because now the door is wide open and Derrick has not only walked through, he's taken up space at the table that's only been me and Taj since my son's birth.

Now Taj is laughing and joking, and though there are no stars in his eyes, there is real admiration for Derrick. This is all my fault. I should've told Taj not to talk to Derrick after the whole heirloom incident. I should've put up a wall faster than the community center went up down the street.

But I don't want Derrick to see how uneasy I am, so I take

a bite of the jambalaya and a moan slips from my lips. My word! How is this so good?

"You like?" Derrick asks, a twinkle of amusement in his eyes.

Right, because I just acted like I do when I eat my favorite chocolate from the chocolatier shop on the boardwalk. "It's amazing. Your mom's recipe?"

"It is. She's originally from New Orleans but settled in Virginia after she got a job there."

"I didn't know that. She doesn't have an accent." I thought everyone from New Orleans had one.

"She never had one because her parents weren't from there, so she talked like they did."

"Where are they from?" Taj asks.

"Texas."

"What about . . ." Taj hesitates.

"Go ahead, man. Ask me whatever."

Really? He's giving my son carte blanche to interrogate him? But I'm not mad, because my insides are actually doing a cheer on the sidelines as my son's shoulders relax.

"What about your dad? You never mention him."

"That's because he didn't want to be a father, so he's never been a part of my life."

"Like mine."

Sympathy crosses Derrick's face, and he leans toward Taj, seriousness replacing the compassion. "I know it's hard not questioning yourself. Thinking you're the reason they didn't want to be around. But you have to remember, that's their baggage. Don't pick up something that was never meant to be yours."

Taj's Adam's apple bobs up and down, and my own throat thickens with unshed tears.

"How do I not?" Taj's voice cracks.

"Because you remember what God says about you. You hold on to the fact that the Creator of the universe took time and care to knit you in your mother's womb. To have such great plans for you. To remember He sings over you. All the things your mom has done for you, God has done and more. That means you were never a mistake. That He created you with intention. And just because your earthly father didn't get a clue of how wonderful you are and what kind of man you'll become, doesn't mean God feels that way. Neither does your mom."

Taj glances at me and I try to curve my mouth upward, but my bottom lip is trying to give away my emotions. I bite the inside of my cheek, willing myself not to tremble.

He turns back to Derrick and slowly nods. "Sometimes I wonder if my mom hadn't had me, maybe she wouldn't be alone now."

"Oh, baby . . ." My heart wrenches at the sadness in his voice.

"Nah, man. Don't think like that. Because then you're forgetting that God's been there for her. Immanuel, God is with us, right?"

Taj nods.

"Not to mention, you've been here brightening her days and showing her what unconditional love is. I bet she doesn't regret a single moment."

"Not a one," I choke out, losing the tether of my emotions. Tears stream silently down my cheeks.

That uneasiness that hit me earlier, that fear that being with Derrick was going to wreck me more than help me has fled. With one little conversation, I'm ready to keep him in our circle forever.

Please, Father, keep him here in Anchor Cove. I want to see where this goes.

Chapter Seventeen

Derrick

Derrick.

My eyes blink open at the sound of my name. The room is dark, so I glance at the digital clock on the nightstand. It reads 5:00 AM. I thought I heard my name, but surely it was a remnant of a dream. I lay my head back down and close my eyes.

Derrick.

I stare up at the ceiling then shift to sitting. No one's in the house and I have that niggling notion in the back of my mind it's God trying to get my attention and the voice I'm hearing isn't some lucid dream. This wouldn't be the first time God has woken me up, but it would be the earliest. I run a hand down my face and blow out a breath, trying to get my mind alert.

If God wants to talk, I definitely want to listen.

Grabbing my Bible, journal, and pen, I head for the porch. I flick the switch for the light and settle into the nearest chair. I draw in a slow inhale then exhale, picturing myself pushing all thoughts out of my head. It helps that I just woke up which means nothing is on my mind right now. Just the memory of my name.

"Speak, Lord," I whisper. "Your servant is listening."

God's voice isn't always audible to me, but when it is, I keep my journal nearby to jot down any pictures He gives me, words I hear, or Bible verses that may speak to more on what God's sharing with me.

A verse comes to mind, so I write it in my notebook.

Psalm 46:10, "Be still, and know that I am God; I will be exalted among the nations, I will be exalted in the earth!"

But that's the last Scripture I know book, chapter, and verse. The rest come in a hurry, and I barely have time to write them before another one pops to mind.

A man's heart plans his way, but the Lord directs his steps.

For My thoughts are not your thoughts, nor are your ways My ways.

Trust in the Lord with all your heart, and lean not on your own understanding; in all your ways acknowledge Him, and He shall direct your paths.

I will instruct you and teach you in the way you should go; I will guide you with My eye.

There are many plans in a man's heart, nevertheless the Lord's counsel—that will stand.

I sit back, staring at the verses that obviously all have a theme. God's telling me His way is the way, and I will know my next step when I need to know it. Obviously, He doesn't always speak to me so cut-and-dry, but even I can see the message right in front of me.

Lord God, I'm so sorry for being impatient. For feeling like You abandoned me. I should've remembered who You are in my heart and not let my circumstances tell me otherwise. I guess I was just scared. Scared that I'll leave here and still have no direction on what to do.

Be still, and know that I am God; I will be exalted among the nations, I will be exalted in the earth!

What does it really mean to be still? I find a site to compare various translations and what they say in the first portion of Psalm 46:10. Besides "be still," there is "cease striving," "stop striving," "let it be and be still," and "stop fighting." The different words all form the same picture. Didn't I say Anchor Cove would be the place I could rest? In the face of wanting answers, I forgot that God told me to rest. To take care of myself. To enjoy life again.

I'd been so focused on finding my next job that I blocked out the *rest*. Also, I've been go, go, go for the past twenty years, that I'm not really sure slowing down has ever been a part of my vocabulary.

I'm sorry I forgot the first part of how You said to rest.

Ignoring the rhythm of rest God put in place isn't good. Sure, I tried my best to take the Sabbath off, unless something work related couldn't be avoided. But outside of that, I didn't do any long periods of rest. Hadn't I told myself the other day that I needed to practice more silence, more stillness? God has my future already mapped out, and He'll let me know each move when I'm ready. That's the truth I have to hold on to regardless of what my eyesight is trying to convey. Regardless of what I want.

I trust You, Lord. You've never steered me wrong. You've never left me alone. You've always cared for me and ensured that I have what I need. Always.

I take a moment to write a prayer of thanksgiving in my journal underneath all the Bible verses. In a minute, I'll look the Scriptures up so I can have the book, chapter, and verse written next to them. I'm sure I've read them before because of how fast they came to mind, but also, if I haven't, I doubt the Holy Spirit needs me to play a hand and can do the work on His own.

Still, by the time I stand to stretch my stiff body, it's a little after six and my stomach lets me know it's time to have breakfast before I go for a run.

When I finally lace up my shoes and jog down the stairs, Simone is coming out of her place dressed in exercise gear as well. I lift a hand in a wave, surprised to see her. Exercising isn't her thing, so why is this the second time she's been out? The first time was when Taj got in an accident and now . . .

I cross the lawn. "Morning."

"Hey, good morning." She swallows. "Why are you up so early?"

"God woke me up. You?"

She sighs. "Insomnia has been waking me early this past week."

My brows rise. "You've been running the *entire* week?"

"Yep. Never thought I'd do something so . . ." Her nose wrinkles. "Not me?"

I laugh. "Yeah. Here I thought this was only your second time."

"No, sir. I'm becoming a regular."

"Care to have some company?"

She bites her lip, studying me from beneath her lashes. "Okay."

We start off slow, and the silence between us stretches. I don't know what's on Simone's mind, but I pray God meets her in the quiet. That she can relax her mind and body and hopefully, get in a catnap later. Just when I've gotten comfortable with the silence, Simone's voice interrupts the quiet with the most unexpected question.

"What did you and Taj talk about yesterday?"

Simone

Derrick trips a little but rights himself quickly.

"You okay?"

"Of course. Just wasn't expecting that. I thought you'd talk about the weather or the waves." He points to the right at the small waves lapping at the shore.

"You don't have to share if you don't want."

"No, I don't mind." He rubs the back of his neck. "But, uh, basically Taj told me I didn't have to impress him. That I didn't have to be nervous about cooking for y'all last night."

"That was sweet of him." Taj is always trying to take pressure off of me and I guess now Derrick.

"Well, actually . . ."

"Uh-oh." I force a laugh, suddenly nervous about what he has to say. "You didn't think it was sweet of him?"

"I wanted him to know he matters. That I realize you and he are a unit, and dating you means I get to have a relationship with Taj as well. I wanted him to know he's important, not just as your son, but because I met him first and genuinely enjoy his company." Derrick shrugs a shoulder as if his words are nonchalant and not rocking the very earth I'm attempting to jog across.

My legs stop moving as they turn to jelly, and I sink onto the nearest bench. I place a hand over my heart, and I'm crying before my mind can even comprehend why.

I came out of my house this morning to essentially run from my emotions. In the beginning, liking Derrick made me cautious. It didn't seem smart to fall for a tourist—still doesn't sound like the best idea. But then I couldn't deny my feelings and Derrick confirmed he was on the same page with me. But this, the sensation in the deepest part of me? I have no words for what it's like.

It's as if I've finally been seen. Heard. *Valued.* And not just me, but also the very son who has had no one but me to be his cheerleader. Derrick sees who Taj is and is becoming and appreciates that. I'm not sure how my son took hearing the sentiment behind Derrick's words, but I'm soaking in just how amazing this man is.

This guy who was supposed to be just passing through has taken up space in my heart and it terrifies me. What will happen if I let down every single guardrail and give him full access? Will he then guard those spaces, or will he come in and wreak havoc like the people before him have?

Derrick kneels before me, wrapping me in his arms while I cry and have an existential crisis about relationships. The irony isn't lost on me. Here I am being held by the very person who's put me in tears in the first place. Not that any of this is his fault. He can't help being so great, and I can't help but be so scared that this relationship could upend every form of protection I've placed around my heart over the years.

When my cries finally stop and I manage to pull myself away from him, the concern in his gaze almost has me tearing right back up.

"What's on your mind?"

"This . . ." I gesture between us. "It feels so . . ." I search for the words, trying to figure out the best way to summarize my emotions.

"Important?"

"Yes." I nod vigorously. "But also, it's like I can't get a handle on my emotions because of the enormity of it all."

Derrick cups my face, gazing right into my eyes. "Simone, I can't tell you what the future holds, but I will tell you I want us to work. Whatever comes our way, I'm committed to making sure it'll improve our relationship."

"Can you be so committed when we've only been on one date?"

Instead of answering me immediately, Derrick takes time to think. "It's not the number of dates that I'm banking on, but the length of time we've known each other and how I feel. Not to mention I have no need to play games. I like you and I want you to know that."

So plain and simple, but I'm grateful that he's honest with me. "Thank you."

He kisses me on the forehead then stands, offering a hand to help me as well. I place my palm against his, loving the warmth and the strength in his hands. When we're standing, staring at one another again, I offer a small smile. Still a little weepy, but happy knowing that none of it scares Derrick away. It's like part of me wants to test the limits just to see if he truly will stick around. The other part doesn't want to rock the boat.

I'm sure I'll find my rhythm the longer we keep seeing each other.

We continue along the boardwalk, and this time, instead of being silent, I share a piece of me that I don't talk about all too often.

"Did you know my water broke with Taj?"

"You mean when you went into labor?"

I nod.

"Were you scared?"

"Terrified." My laugh flies freely in the air. It's easy to joke about now, but I remember the fear when that pop sounded and fluid from my body went everywhere. "I was in the laundry room trying to wash some of the baby clothes I'd received. The church had welcomed me with open arms and threw me a baby shower."

"Wow. That's amazing."

I nod. "I assumed they'd judge me, but one of the ladies took me under her wing. Mrs. Reese. She's the one who arranged the shower and assigned people to bring food. She had all these different games planned. She was also the first person to babysit Taj for me."

"I'm glad you found support here."

"Same. I'm not sure what life would've been like if I kept facing rejection like I did back home."

"What did you do once your water broke?"

"Called Mrs. Reese. I was sobbing and telling her all the things I hadn't managed to complete on my to-do list, and she convinced me to grab some towels and drive to the hospital."

Derrick lets out a low whistle. "That's a lot. Did she go with you to the hospital?"

"Yes, she did." I look up into the bright sky. "She had me pack a bag a couple of weeks prior, so I was able to grab that and go to the hospital. She met me there and kept me calm throughout the whole delivery."

"How long was your delivery?"

"Ten hours. Taj was born at three in the morning the following day."

"Wow. You're amazing."

I glance over and see the sincerity on Derrick's face. Admiration shines in his eyes and heat rises to my cheeks. It seems unusual to feel pride in something that women have been doing since the beginning of time, but the awe on Derrick's face reminds me that *I* brought life into the world. With the blessing and grace of God, Taj was born perfectly healthy and my body was the vessel used to birth him. That *is* amazing.

"I've always focused on Taj and the miracle that is his life, but I've never really thought about my role in it."

"You should. He wouldn't be the outstanding young man he is without your love and guidance. That's something to thank God for. You had a hand in that and there's nothing wrong with taking pleasure in that."

"Thank you, Derrick." He's always got me looking at life from a different perspective, and I can't help but love that he's a natural encourager. If only I could be that kind of person for him. Then perhaps he wouldn't beat himself up so much for not knowing what's coming next.

Chapter Eighteen

Derrick

I tighten the light bulb in the ceiling of the church's kitchen. Pastor David called me yesterday to ask if I would do some work around the building. Since I finished painting Simone's rental, which is now occupied, I jumped at the chance to stay active.

"There you are."

I peer down the ladder into the face of the man I was just thinking of. "Hey, Pastor."

"Please, call me David."

Poor man. I don't have the heart to tell him my mama would skin me alive for calling a pastor by his first name. "Did you need me for something?" Ask a direct question and I get to avoid the issue of what to call him.

"Yes. I wanted to ask you for a favor. But let me just tell you, you don't have to answer right away. You can take some time to think and pray about it first."

"All right. I'm listening."

He forges ahead. "So, every year we take the teen boys camping. It's a time to get a little mentorship from the older gentlemen and bond as a congregation. Unfortunately, two of my men have backed out, so I'm looking for replacements. I thought of you and . . ." His voice trails off.

"Appreciate you thinking of me."

"Taj goes every year." There's a twinkle in the pastor's eyes, as if he knows what adding that little bit of information will do.

And it's pretty effective, because now I'm interested. "When do you need to know by?"

"Tuesday, if possible."

I nod.

"Okay then. I'll let you get back to it."

"Thanks for the work. I appreciate it."

"Of course." He regards me thoughtfully. "May I ask you a question?"

"Sure."

"You running from something?"

"More like trying to decide what my future holds."

Pastor David's head tilts. "You know, 'a man's heart plans his way, but the Lord directs his steps.'"

"Proverbs 16:9." I shake my head in bemusement. "The Lord recently brought that to mind."

"Sounds like He's trying to tell you something."

"Oh, He brought up a whole bunch of Scriptures that drove in the truth that He'll direct me. But . . ." I pause. I didn't come here to bother Pastor David. He hired me to do a job, not talk about my problems.

"But what?" He slides his hands into his khaki short pockets like he has all the time in the world.

"But how much is dependent on me doing the work? On actually taking steps forward? It feels silly to simply sit and wait for God to do something. The whole faith without works, you know?"

"Sure. There's definitely a time where faith with works is

a necessary part of our spiritual journey. But what if God specifically tells you to rest? What if He specifically tells you to slow down? Is not doing anything silly then?"

"Uh . . ."

Pastor David arches a brow. "If you've been told to rest and you're not, what would you call that?"

Heat crawls up my neck. "Sounds disobedient."

"Hmm. So why would you disobey God?" He holds up a hand, stopping his own line of questioning. "First, *did* God tell you to rest?"

"He did give me the 'Be still and know' verse when I had some quiet time the other day. But the rest of the verses were more about not trying to understand but letting Him guide me."

Pastor David nods slowly as if he's contemplating everything I've said. Maybe he's giving the Spirit time to work and reveal things to him. I don't know. The silence isn't awkward, though, so I wait patiently for him to say something profound.

"Sounds like God wants you to stop searching for the next step, for the next answer, not necessarily telling you to be physically still. So, the question you have to ask yourself is if your work is you trying to find an answer." He gives me a pointed stare.

I laugh, because what else can I do? "I get it."

"I hope you do."

"I think I've had enough hints from the Lord to get what He's saying."

"Good." Pastor David rocks back on the balls of his feet. "One more thing, Derrick."

"Yes, sir?" Hanging around locals in Anchor Cove has made hearing my first name more normal. For twenty years, I went by my last name of Benjamin in the military crowd.

"Trust Him. He never steers us in the wrong direction. *Never.*"

He's right. God has always taken care of me. Whenever I listen to what He says, I've been able to thank the Lord down the road. Whenever I didn't listen, regret and repentance came. Just because I don't have the answers on my own timing doesn't negate that I can trust God. He's faithful. Steadfast. *True.* Which means I *will* trust Him and His plan for me.

"Thank you. I needed that reminder."

"Good. Don't forget to praise Him in the waiting. And if you can, wait joyfully."

Man, Pastor David isn't holding any punches. "Yes, sir."

He grins then shuffles out of the room like we didn't just have a profound conversation. Perhaps our chat doesn't impact the pastor the way it does me. After all, his business is in the spiritual realm. But I can already tell the difference in my heart. I'm lighter, unburdened, and ready to praise the Lord.

As I complete the task Pastor David hired me for, I sing worship songs under my breath, whistle when I don't remember the words, and pray when my spirit needs to bow before the Lord. At the end of the day, I've got a pep to my step that hasn't been there in a long time.

Not only that, but all I'm able to think of is how much I missed Simone and Taj. Not hearing Taj's random talking points or seeing Simone's glowing face means I'm itching to stop by their place even if it's just to lay eyes on them. I don't need Simone to feed me. I don't need Taj to hang out with me. I simply want to see them.

Lord, should I do the mentoring trip?

It's not something I have to strive to do. I wouldn't say yes because I have some misguided belief that I'm going to be a youth pastor or anything like that. But the idea of hanging out with Taj and bonding . . . that makes me pause.

After quieting my mind and listening for God's voice, I make a U-turn and head back into church and let Pastor David know I'd be happy to go on the camping trip.

Simone

I fold the T-shirt, smoothing down the edges so they're nice and flat.

"I cannot believe you're folding my laundry." Amy's flat on her back, resting on the sofa.

"It's not like you can do it, and your husband has to work." Amy and her kids caught a bad stomach bug. When I called to check on her, she was crying about the number of times she's upchucked and the state of her house.

She'd also been concerned about the baby, but her doctor assured her she'd be fine. I brought some Pedialyte and have been cleaning the place from top to bottom.

"Still. Folding my laundry. My unmentionables are in there," she grouses.

"What century are you from?" I chuckle, shaking my head. "Unmentionables."

"We're friends and I love you to death, but I may never recover from you folding my underwear."

"When you see how neat your underwear drawer looks after I'm done, you may actually thank me."

She snorts. "Not likely. It'll take me at least another decade of friendship before I can ever look you in the eye again."

I pry her arm from her forehead, and when her eyelids

pop open, make sure to stare intently into her gaze. But she's not lying about being embarrassed, because she looks away quickly, her face flushing red.

"Poor baby. You'll survive the humiliation."

"Says you."

We say nothing more as I continue to fold her clothes. Then sniffles reach my ears. I turn to study my friend, and when I see tears slide down her face, I hold back a sigh. I hurt for Amy, but other than cleaning her house, I'm not sure what I can do.

"You okay?" I ask quietly.

"I hate crying because of pregnancy hormones, but it's even more aggravating when it's because I'm so sick I can't do my own laundry."

"Sweetie, does anyone want to do their laundry?"

"No," she chokes out.

"If I agree not to touch any . . . unmentionables, will that make you feel better?"

"Yes." She sniffs.

I reach for the box of tissues on her end table and pass them along. "Here. I won't touch them."

"Thanks, Simone." Amy blows long and hard into the tissue then cleans her nose. "Catch me up on your life. Mine is sad and full of vomit. Surely yours has to be better."

I grin. "The bar's on the floor."

"I know." She flops her arm back across her forehead. "Tell me what's going on with you and Derrick. Have you kissed? Are you dating? What's up?"

"Take a breath, goodness."

She laughs softly, as if the effort took all of her energy.

"We've seen each other every day. Part of me is nervous about what happens when he leaves, but the other part wants to be here for every moment."

"Are you afraid he'll leave and never return?"

"Something like that." After all, my family ditched me, and my first boyfriend fled after learning about Taj. Nothing about me makes people stick around.

"But what about Derrick says that he leaves in hard times? He literally retired from the military, meaning he gave something his time and commitment. And from what you said, he never dated because he didn't want to let his wife be alone. Kinda admirable in a fall on your sword type of way."

I huff at the image. "I know I shouldn't be scared, but I am."

"Whoa. I'm not saying don't be scared. I'm saying look at who Derrick is. Look at what he's showing you. And whenever you get scared, remind yourself who he is."

"You're right." I let out an exhale. Derrick is so good, and I've been worrying that means he has to be hiding something. But is it possible God is simply blessing me with a good guy? Even if I had to wait until I was thirty-three years old to find him.

"I am." Amy sounds smug, but since her face is still pale, I'll let her have this win. "When do you see him again?"

"Hopefully whenever I go home. It's been weird not talking to him all day."

"Aww, you really like him."

I can't help but smile. It takes over my face before playing it cool even enters my mind. "I do, Ames. He's so . . . so *steady*. It's like nothing fazes him. And when he shows emotion, instead of panicking, I want to be steady for him." I bite my lip and stare at my friend. "Is that weird?"

"No, babe. That's what a real partnership looks like. It's not fifty-fifty. It's both of you giving your all. And when one can't, the other picks up the slack. And when it flips the other way, then you do the reverse. You celebrate the highs together and you be there when a low hits either one of you."

"I don't know what that looks like. My mom always let my dad dominate. And when he wanted me gone, she didn't disagree. She never disagreed with him."

"That's not healthy. Have you and Derrick had an argument yet?"

I shake my head.

"Well, don't worry if you haven't. But whenever you do, pay attention to how he argues and how you do. It'll let you know if there are behaviors you need to correct and vice versa. I had to learn to argue with Chris."

"What do you mean?" There's a right way to argue?

"I always threw everything back in his face. I remembered every past argument, every issue we ever had, and used it for fuel." She sighs. "I got counseling at church, and one of the things they had us do was study 1 Corinthians 13. It talks about not keeping a record of wrongs and I realized that every time I argued with my husband, I was going against the very thing God teaches about love. It made me look at things differently."

"Wow. The only one I have to argue with is Taj. I've tried to do that differently than how my parents taught me, but it's not the same dynamic at all."

"It's not. But you'll figure it out. If you and Derrick are meant to be together for life, you'll find your own rhythm and way of communicating that works for the both of you. But it doesn't work unless it's equally beneficial."

"Okay." I gather the folded shirts and stand. "Thanks for the tip. Now take a nap for me, 'kay?"

"Already dreaming."

Chapter Nineteen

Derrick

An incoming call flashing *Mom* across the screen lights my phone up.

"Hey. How are you feeling?" I set my library book down on the end table.

After Pastor David asked me to go on the camping trip, I grabbed a mentoring book from the Anchor Cove Library. I'm halfway through and already a little more steadied, believing I won't actually ruin this opportunity.

You did lead people in the military. This time they're a little younger.

"I told you I'm fine. My wrist is healing nicely."

"You're taking it easy?" I know her. Mom doesn't like to rest. Or maybe it's that she doesn't know how to. *Ha.* Guess I know who I got it from.

"Of course, son. But I didn't call to talk about me."

I shake my head in amusement. "What did you call to talk about?"

"Your neighbor."

I sit back in the chair. "Simone or Taj?"

"Both, actually."

"I'm listening." What could she possibly be thinking regarding those two?

"Are you seeing Simone?"

The urge to respond like a smart aleck has a quip on my tongue, but I battle it back down. "Yes."

An audible sigh fills the line. "Son . . ."

"What?" I recognize that tone. I've heard her say "son" that way when she's disappointed in my actions and believes I should behave differently. "Why do you make us being together sound like a bad thing?"

"She's a single mom."

"I know. I've met Taj and I like him. He's a good kid."

"You of all people should know how precarious dating a single woman is. That boy probably looks up to you, and if you break his mom's heart, you're breaking his as well."

I squeeze my eyes shut. "Don't you think I've thought of this? Do you think so little of me that I wouldn't have factored this in before I asked her out?"

"No. But I also don't think you considered all of the ramifications. He's a teenage boy and will be leaving the house soon. If you break her heart, you may keep him at home the rest of his life. He'll believe he has to watch over and take care of her."

I frown. "Mom, is that the reason you never dated? You thought I'd have to take care of you or something?"

"Thought? You did! You were always asking me how you could help. You watched my every move, trying to circumvent any disaster. I had to kick your behind out to the military just to give you someone else to look out for."

It's possible she nudged me in the Air Force's direction, but I don't think it was as bad as she's making it out to be.

"Mom, come on."

"No. That young woman is lovely. Her son is bright. If

you bond with them this summer and leave, what do you think that'll do? You're impacting a family, not just a person, Derrick."

"I know," I say softly.

"Then you should know what you have to do next."

I'm not going to argue with my mother right now, though every line of reasoning is waiting in my mind. Instead, I end the call with a *goodbye* and stare unseeingly.

Starting a relationship with Simone seemed like a God-blessed endeavor. I've made sure to factor in Taj and ensure he knows he matters to me as well. I've been intentional with Simone and letting her know that this isn't just a summer fling for me. I want more with her.

What if my mom is right? I don't know what the future holds. Does that mean heartache awaits? If God gave me the green light to date this wonderful woman, won't He ensure the ending will be a happy one? One where we're all together and have each other's backs until the Lord calls us home?

Now doubts replace the reassurance that was there before. I don't know if I should cancel my date with Simone or keep it. Do I need to break up with her at some point during the date?

I run a hand down my face. Boy, did my mother really mess with my confidence. She means well, but now I wish I never answered her phone call.

My head drops back onto the chair, and I let out a sigh. *Lord, what do I do? Didn't You tell me to take a leap of faith with Simone? If so, how can I be so tangled up inside now?*

I check my watch and realize I'm running out of time. If I'm going to keep my date, then I need to change out of my shirt and gym shorts and into something better. We're going on a dinner cruise tonight, so I'll dress up a little more than I have on our previous dates.

Twenty minutes later, I knock on Simone's door. When it opens, my breath catches. Simone's a vision in a pale-yellow summer dress that makes her skin glow.

"Wow."

Her lips curve into a smile. "Wow yourself." Her finger points at me, going up and down. "This is lethal."

I laugh. "No, ma'am. You're the one trying to make me lose my breath."

She's trying to keep a smile at bay but her lips tilt just enough for me to notice she's pleased.

"You ready?" I ask.

"Mm-hm." She locks the door and we walk to my Jeep. I hold open the door and my stomach dips as I think about the evening before us. I'm no clearer on what I should do. Is shoving my mom's conversation out of my head the best thing or should I consider her advice and take the wisdom she's offering?

"You okay?" Simone asks, pulling me from my thoughts.

Tell her. Talk it out.

But my whole body tenses at the idea. "A lot on my mind." I put the Jeep in reverse then into Drive as we head toward the marina.

"Anything you want to talk about?"

"Not right now, but maybe later." Hopefully by then, I'll have the words.

Simone

Derrick has been quiet all evening. *Too* quiet. But since our server is currently giving us our second course, I'll hold my tongue. For now.

God, please be in the midst of this conversation.

Because I can't *stay* silent. I need to know what's going on in his head. I have a hint it has something to do with our relationship.

"I have a hypothetical question," I say after the server leaves.

"Oh yeah? What is it?"

"Say you get a job in Denver."

Derrick's lips curve into a half smile. The look is so adorable, I want to reach over and run my thumb across his bottom lip. I blink, trying to focus and remember the purpose of my question.

"Wait." He waves a hand. "Why Denver?"

"First city that popped in my head."

"Okay. Go on."

"All right. So, you move to Denver at the end of the summer. What happens to us? Would we say goodbye and that's it?" I barely get the question out, nerves giving me chills all of a sudden.

"No," he says slowly. "That wouldn't be it."

Thank You, Lord. I let out a discreet exhale. "Long-distance, then?" I watch, waiting for any kind of tell, any kind of hint to what he's thinking.

Derrick reaches across the table and intertwines his fingers with mine. I try not to cling to him, but I like us. I like where this relationship is going, but I don't know what's going to happen at the end of the summer. The days are passing by, whether I want them to or not.

"Is that something you'd want?" Derrick asks.

"I'd be willing to try." I won't plead with Derrick, but I do want to know we're on the same page.

"I'm glad. I've never thought of long-distance because, selfishly, I want you near me. But that would give us time to come up with a better solution." Derrick pauses, his thumb creating circles on the back of my hand. "Would you ever consider leaving Anchor Cove?"

I almost let go of his hand. Not because I'm repulsed but because the shock going through me is overwhelming. Leave Anchor Cove? It's never even crossed my mind. My friends are here. My son's friends are here. How could I just yank Taj from school before he graduates?

"No, never mind." Derrick shakes his head. "Taj hasn't even graduated high school yet, so it makes no sense."

I swallow, hating that I didn't respond. Tears of relief are pricking at my eyes, wanting to make an appearance. *Say something*. "Wow. I never saw myself in Denver."

Derrick snorts but even though it's not his usual low tenor chuckle, I'll count it as a win because the tension is already diffusing.

"*I've* never seen myself in Denver. What do people do there? Bond with nature?"

"Cute. They probably ski on vacations and walk outside without a jacket if it's fifty degrees."

This time I get Derrick's usual laugh and my heart settles back into my chest and out of my throat. Still, my fingers tremble a little as I untangle our hands and reach for my glass of ice water. The cold refreshment does nothing to soothe the ache in my throat. Somehow, asking my hypothetical made our date take a turn I wasn't fully prepared for.

Derrick changes the subject and soon we're laughing again. We're learning more about each other's likes and dislikes and our relationship is growing. But in the back of my head, I'm wondering where this ends. With me and my son heartbroken and alone in Anchor Cove, or will a miracle happen, and Derrick get a sustainable job here?

I know which choice I desire, but life hasn't gone the way

I've wanted for so long, I'm not sure hoping for a better outcome is smart.

Lord God, help my unbelief.

The Lord is a good God. I believe that truth mentally, but I'm afraid to tell Him all I hope for with Derrick. What if He tells me no? And seeing Derrick's smiling face across from me right now, doing something as simple as holding hands, laughing at each other's jokes, it fills me with so much joy. I can't remember the last time euphoria wrapped around me like a warm blanket but also lit my nerves on fire with attraction. I didn't have this giddiness with my first boyfriend.

As we dig our spoons into the shared dessert, I stare into Derrick's dark eyes. "I really like you," I whisper.

I'm not sure why I said it so quietly. But the setting sun, the lull of the boat, the white lights creating a romantic atmosphere, it all has me not wanting to disrupt the bubble we're currently living in.

"And I probably like you more," Derrick says in the same tone, as if afraid to disturb the mood as well.

What do we do about it? How can I watch you leave when the summer ends?

I don't want to look beyond the glow of the moment. There will be days ahead of me where a decision will *have* to be made. But it's not today, not on our date. So, I don't bring up my hypothetical back up again. Not when the boat docks. Not when Derrick drives me home.

It isn't until Derrick cups my face and begins to lean forward that I realize the position in which I've found myself. I place a hand over his heart and halt his movement.

He immediately straightens, dark eyes finding mine, searching for the answer to why I stopped him. I lick my lips, trying to gather the courage to be honest. But the care in his gaze has me squeezing my eyes shut.

"I'm afraid if I let you kiss me, then when summer ends, I'll be devastated." The words seem too loud in the night air, but I can't take them back.

Only when Derrick's hand leaves my face and cool air drifts over me, do I open my eyes. Whatever I thought I'd see isn't there.

Derrick nods in understanding and then gives me a small smile. "See you tomorrow?"

I bite my lip and nod. I do want to see him as much as I also want to hold on to something that will keep me from being shattered come Labor Day.

Chapter Twenty

Derrick

SOMEHOW, I'VE FOUND MYSELF IN THE MIDDLE OF JULY. I have about six weeks left on my rental before I need to return to Virginia where Mom is or hopefully move on to whatever life has in store for me next. Since God gave me those verses—ones I've been repeating to myself on a daily basis—I've done better about not being in a constant state of panic. On the flip side, the conversation I had with Simone last week put me back on the seesaw of begging God, trusting God, and begging Him some more.

Still, I don't know what will happen after Labor Day, which means I'm forced to pretend that nothing is bothering me every time I see Simone and Taj. And now I'm packing one of the church's vans with everyone's duffel bags for the camping trip. One of the other chaperones—Cam?—is handing me the bags as I attempt to Tetris the back of the van with everyone's luggage. So far so good, but we might run out of room.

"Last one," Maybe-Cam says.

"Thanks." I place the green bag in the righthand corner and step back to survey my handiwork.

"Not bad, man."

I nod.

"Which one is yours?" he asks, pointing to the teens.

"Oh, uh, I don't have kids." I point to Taj. "But Taj and I are friends and I'm dating his mom so . . ." Why does this seem so awkward?

"Gotcha. Well, those two are mine." He points to what appears to be identical twins. "Sam and Graham."

That's it. I'm definitely cementing his name as Cam. No way this *am* is a coincidence. "How old are they?"

"Fourteen as of last month. How old is your . . . friend?"

"Fifteen." Where will I be then? Will I be able to celebrate with him and Simone? Or will Simone and I have ended our relationship by then?

Don't think those thoughts. Trust the Lord for today and leave tomorrow to Him too.

"Oh, cool. I've seen him around. He seems like a good kid."

"The best."

"I think it's amazing you're joining him on this trip. Were you trying to earn brownie points or legitimately wanting to camp?"

I force out a laugh. "Pastor David asked me to chaperone before I even knew who was attending. But I did agree so we could hang out. Taj is a great kid."

"That's awesome, man." Cam claps me on the shoulder just as Pastor David calls for us to gather around.

I follow Cam into the circle the teens and chaperones make.

"Listen up. I'll be giving the chaperones four kids each to watch over. Teens, do not attempt to ditch your chaperone. The purpose of this trip is to bond with one another, but also to learn. This is your chance to ask the questions you want answers to. We'll have small group time with your chaperone but also campfire time with everyone so that the wisdom is shared. Any questions?"

No one raises their hand.

"Great. Listen for your name and your chaperone's name." Pastor David begins to list names, and I tune him out until he says my name. "Chaperone Derrick Benjamin will be with Taj Avery, Nate Conner, Asher Jones, and Hakeem Smith."

The boys all come stand by me.

Taj grins ear-to-ear and leans close to whisper to me. "You'll be sick of me by the time the weekend is finished."

I fold my arms and bend toward him. "Or vice versa. It's all fun and games until the fun guy has to be the chaperone."

Taj laughs, the pitch loud and a little high, reminding me just how young he still is. Regardless, I'm looking forward to hanging out with the kid along with the other three. I make sure to introduce myself as soon as Pastor David finishes grouping us all.

"Are you Taj's stepdad?" Hakeem asks.

Taj groans.

"I'm his friend."

"But you're dating his mom, right?" Hakeem asks.

"Is that your business?" Taj grouses.

I lay a hand on his arm. "For the purpose of this trip, I'm Taj's friend. You can call me Derrick or Benjamin. I answer to both."

"Why?" Nate asks.

"I was in the military for twenty years and they call you by your last name, so sometimes I forget who this Derrick person is."

The boys chuckle at my attempt at humor.

"Shall we load up?"

They all nod. We've been assigned to van number one. The boys go in first, and I follow. There's a lot of chatter on the way to the campsite, and though I expected Taj to speak to most of the other kids, he keeps up a steady stream of conversation with me.

"What do you think my mom is up to?"

"Probably has her feet up, face mask on, and a drink in her hand," I quip.

"Yeah right." Taj slaps his knee. "More like her phone in her hand looking at the tracker app to see where I'm at."

"You don't think she and Amy are having a girls' night celebrating no kids around?"

"Actually, that's plausible. Amy's feeling better now."

I'm still surprised Simone took the time to watch over her friend by cleaning her whole house. What a woman.

Lord, please let us stay together forever. I know I keep asking You that, but she's perfect.

"What do you think she'll do when I go to college?" Taj's voice has lost its glee, and he sounds more contemplative.

"You mean on a daily basis or the simple fact that you're gone?"

"That I'm gone. Do you think she'll be sad?"

"Definitely. It's been you two for fifteen years. She'll miss you like crazy."

He lets out a forlorn sigh. "I'll miss her too. But I gotta grow up sometime, right?"

"She'll always be there for you. No matter where you are. That's how my mom is, and I know yours will be there for you too."

"Did you miss your mom when you joined the military?"

"Definitely." Just thinking about it makes me want to laugh. "I was scared spitless. But the military turned me into a man. I've been able to visit my mom as often as I want, and she's visited me as well. Our relationship isn't the same as when I was a kid, but that's part of growing up."

"Yeah, I get that. I just wish that when I graduate, I won't have to leave her alone."

The heat of Taj's stare might as well burn the side of my face off. Like the man I claimed the military made me, I turn to meet his gaze head on.

"Maybe you won't. But that's not something I can guarantee right now. I hope you know that."

"I mean, yeah. You've only known her for a short time. I just thought I'd put that idea out there. In case you've never considered long-term."

"I have. I didn't enter our relationship thinking it would only be for the summer."

"But you don't know what'll happen with your job."

"Exactly."

Taj and I exhale twin sighs. I won't ask the Lord for help again. Not because I can't, but because He's heard every prayer. He knows the situation. And He's asked me to trust. So that's what I'm going to do.

Simone

Taj has camped every year with the church since he turned thirteen. But there's something about knowing he's there with Derrick this year that changes the whole dynamic. Suddenly, I'm thinking of the reality of our relationship. If Derrick and I were to go the distance, he would become my son's stepfather. The word *stepfather* does this weird reverberation in my head as I try to wrap my mind around the thought.

If Derrick and I were married right now, Taj *would* be

camping with his stepfather. The thing is, I can perfectly visualize Derrick in that role. That's why the what-ifs of his job have me tangled in a knot so much. He's such a good man and I'd be lucky to do life with him.

Then why does it only have to be in Anchor Cove?

The question convicts me. Frankly, it's been echoing in the back of my head since I brought up the topic on our cruise date. When I listed Taj's high school years and friends as a reason to stay, I wasn't making up excuses. While those are very real factors, if I consider Derrick as the one I want to go the distance with, then wouldn't I want to move heaven and earth to be with him?

Guess the question is how much do you care about him?

I've only known him for about seven weeks. We've only been dating for almost three weeks. Is that enough time to know if I want to be with him forever? Yet the thought of him leaving Anchor Cove at the end of the summer wrenches my gut. I wish a decision didn't have to be made so soon.

Or it doesn't, and I just haven't figured out an alternate option yet.

Hence the reason I'm taking time to simply be and think about our relationship and what I'm experiencing. I'd love to bask in that warm glow of being attracted to another person without having to worry about the rest. But life waits for no one and Derrick arrived with a ticking clock following behind him.

My phone vibrates against the table, and I glance at the screen to see who's calling. It shouldn't be Derrick or Taj, but if something happened . . . My mind still hasn't forgotten Taj's accident.

But the number is unknown. It doesn't appear to be a scam call. Perhaps it's someone interested in a rental.

I slide my thumb across the screen to accept the call. "Hi, this is Simone Avery. How may I help you?"

Silence greets my ear. I pull the phone away and see my bars are all there and the call hasn't dropped.

"Hello?" I say.

"Simone?"

Everything within me stills at the sound of my mother's voice. "M-mama?" The word comes out shaky, or maybe it's my body that's shaking. I can't tell past the rushing in my ears or the thudding of my heart.

"It's been a while."

Uh . . . Duh. But my brain can't seem to form words.

"How have you been, Simone?"

"Are you *really* starting with small talk?"

Breathe, girl. This is not the tone you want to start off with.

But too many years of hurt have been stored up in my heart. I thought I made sure to do the work of forgiveness, but this intense heat filling my face and the balled-up fist pounding my thigh says otherwise. I. Am. *Livid.*

How can she call here and make random small talk as if we'd merely lost touch instead of her kicking me out of the house and forbidding me from coming back?

"I really didn't know how to start the conversation. I . . ." A sigh fills my ear.

As much as I don't want to sympathize, a little prick of awareness breaks through the red haze.

"Why are you calling?"

"I never meant to let so many years pass us by. And now . . ." She sniffs. Her crying is audible, and a pinprick of sympathy has turned into my eyes watering.

I'm barely holding back my own sniffling when my mother speaks again.

"I'm so sorry, baby. I did you and your son such a disservice."

I want to hear her apology, but I also want to hang up the phone and pretend like this never happened. A tiny voice keeps encouraging me to keep my heart soft and listen to the outpouring of emotion coming from my mom. But what I thought were weeds of hurt are actually roots of bitterness. I pull the cell phone away from my ear and hit the red button. Immediately the call ends, silencing her voice.

I'm not sure how long I hold my phone or how long I cry, but when I blink again, it's dark outside and I'm shivering. Somehow, hours have passed while my heart breaks all over again.

I should talk to God about the conversation with my mom. I know the bitterness that's been uncovered should be laid at His feet. But right now, I don't want the Lord to tell me to forgive and I don't want to have any sympathy toward my mother.

Instead, I get up and pad down the hallway to my bed. Taj won't be back for another day and a half. I crawl under the covers and close my eyes, pretending like the day never happened.

Chapter Twenty-One

Derrick

It's our last night of campfire discussions. I settle onto the stump and balance my plate on my thigh. I've got two hot dogs, a bag of chips, and the stuff to make s'mores once I finish my dinner. Taj settles next to me with the same offerings, only he has four hot dogs.

After a few minutes of eating, Pastor David clears his throat. "All right, men. Tonight's topic is our emotions."

The teens start groaning, and I stifle a laugh.

"I know, I know, I *know*. Believe me. We don't talk about those things, or at least society says we can't. But what does the Bible say?" He looks at every one of us around the campfire.

Some of the teens shift uneasily in their seats, but Nate raises his hand.

"Nate, what does the Bible say?"

"Um, it doesn't say anything."

"Are you sure?"

Another kid raises his hand. "I mean, the Psalms are kind of about emotion."

"Excellent, Jacob. Would y'all agree with that assessment?" the pastor asks.

Taj raises his hand. "I would. King David poured out his feelings, like in Psalm 23 when he talks about walking 'through the valley of the shadow of death,' you can sense the anguish, you know?"

I smile at him. He's such a smart kid and has a lot of insight. Our small group talks and the campfire discussions have taught me just how much Taj has been soaking in. His understanding of faith and who God is and who God's developing Taj into is astounding. Simone would be proud.

"Excellent, Taj. So why do we men think we can't have feelings?"

"Because social media tells us not to," Hakeem blurts out. "I've seen ladies say a guy who cries gives them the ick."

Some of the other teens nod in agreement. My heart hurts for them. I didn't have a pervasive social media experience like they do. I got my first cell phone when I joined the Air Force. I only bought one then because I wanted a way to talk to my mom no matter where the military sent me. Which also meant that social media accounts didn't come until later.

"What does God say about emotions? If King David modeled for us that they exist, that we have them, and we can go to God with them, what does the Lord say about feelings?"

Asher's hand shoots up. I'm surprised. He's been pretty quiet most of the weekend, but I'm hopeful he's starting to be comfortable around the rest of us.

"Asher, what are your thoughts?"

"Well, God is love. And God made us in His image so that means we should be love. It's why it's one of the fruits of the Spirit. The fruits are actions, but they're also emotions. I think God made emotions for us to experience them and react to them. It's up to us whether we're going to react holy like Him or not." He frowns. "Well, maybe not solely up to us. We have the Holy Spirit to help us."

"Wow, I love the insight of recognizing who God is and that He made us in His image, which means we share common attributes. Pointing out the fruit of the Spirit is a great example of emotion. Have we seen any other emotions listed in regard to God?"

This time I put a hand in the air.

"Derrick."

"God is a jealous God."

"But isn't jealousy bad?" John asks. He's the pastor's son and you can tell. Not just by looks, but by temperament and knowledge.

I'm glad he asked this question because it used to trip me up.

"Nah, not jealous in a bad way," Taj jumps in to answer. "But like in the way you want to guard someone. He is the only God so having idols in our lives ruins our relationship with Him. Sort of like married couples—they'd be jealous if their spouse put anyone else before them, because it messes with the marriage covenant."

We continue our discussion, and little by little, hands stop lifting and the boys just speak freely. By the end, I think we all believe we can be freer with our emotions, knowing that God experiences them as well and placed them in us for a reason.

Once the boys are all in their tents for the night, the chaperones gather around the campfire once more.

Pastor David looks around and asks, "How do you think the trip is going so far?"

"This has been a fantastic experience," Tommy answers. "My son's really connecting with the other kids, and it's been a blessing to see him connect with God as well."

"Totally agree," Ron says. "I'll continue doing this every year just to see my kid click with the Word the way he has this weekend."

"What about you, Derrick?" Pastor David stares straight at me.

I'm trying not to squirm, but it's like a spotlight is beating down on me. "I'm enjoying myself and it's been great to see Taj in this element too."

"I've seen the way you connect with the boys. I've had quite a few come up to thank me for putting them in your group."

I blink, too stunned to do anything else. Was it Nate? Asher? Hakeem? Regardless, I can't help but feel some kind of way. "Wow."

"We'd love to have you next year."

"I'll keep that in mind."

When we return home tomorrow, I'll miss the trip and the many ways we've all gone deeper in the Word and got to know one another. I'm marking this down as a plus in the find a way to stay in Anchor Cove forever column. Hopefully, I remind myself that the Lord could still send me somewhere else. I don't want to hold too tightly to the idea of only being here, even though that's what I want. I guess time will tell what will happen.

Simone

"Mom, I'm home."

Taj's voice reaches the kitchen where I've been cooking dinner to feed him and Derrick when they returned.

Anything to distract my mind from replaying the conversation with my mother.

"In the kitchen." I turn the dial to low and wipe my hands on the dishrag before moving toward the living room.

Before I even leave the doorway, Taj stands in front of me, a huge grin on his face. His face is browner, and he smells like campfire, but seeing him brings instant joy. I open my arms and he walks right into them. He squeezes me tight then lets go.

"Have a good time?"

"We had an amazing time. Right, D?" He glances over his shoulder and Derrick steps closer.

My heart picks up speed. I want to hug him like I did Taj. Okay actually, I want to do more than a little hugging. Except I'm the one who asked him not to kiss me unless he's staying in Anchor Cove. Still, after not seeing him for a few days, that rule seems incredibly rude.

"Right." Derrick meets my gaze, and something electric passes between us.

Did he miss me as much as I missed him? "Taj, go put your luggage away."

"Yes, ma'am."

As soon as he leaves the room, the space between Derrick and me evaporates. He pulls me close, tucking me under his chin, and I sigh at the contact. How does this man feel like home in so short of a time?

"Missed you," he murmurs.

"I missed you too." I pull back to peer up at him and my gaze drops to his full lips. Once again, I wonder if I'll find his beard scratchy or . . .

"Can't keep looking at me like that and expect me to keep my hands to myself, Simone." Derrick's hands span my back, pulling me closer.

As if there was any space between us. I barely hear his words over the drumming of my heart.

"Simone . . ." he whispers.

We say nothing more because I've risen on my toes to kiss him.

His lips are soft, and my skin heats with the touch. Derrick's hands slowly move around my waist, up my arms, until one cups the side of my face while the other grips the back of my head. He takes over the kiss, deepening it in a way that makes me thankful he has a firm grip on me because my legs are floating. *I'm* floating. Barely tethered to the ground from the sensation he creates in me.

Derrick breaks contact, our breathing ragged between us. I don't want to meet his gaze, because now I know. This is so much more than I've ever imagined. My heart holds a happiness I want to protect with all my heart. Yet if God calls Derrick somewhere else, and I'm left behind, I don't know how I'll handle it.

I wrap my arms around myself and step back.

"Hey, hey." He reaches for me, rubbing my arms. "What's going on? What are you thinking?"

"Derrick, maybe we should—"

"Hey, Mom, did you make—" Taj freezes as he takes in my wary expression and Derrick's concerned one. "Um, I think I should go back to my room."

"Nah. Grab yourself a plate. We'll go out back and talk for a moment." Derrick tugs my hand and leads me out to the backyard. After assisting me into a chair, he pulls the matching one close so we're facing one another. "Talk to me."

"What are we doing?"

"Dating."

"To what purpose?" I wait to hear what he has to say.

"Simone, I'm hoping this leads to vows and us being on

the same team for the rest of our lives. I promise I wouldn't date you just to pass the time. I'm not trying to mess with your heart."

But he is. I want so much from him. What if he can't give it to me? What if he fails me?

Humans fail each other. It's inevitable.

That may be so, but I don't know if my heart can handle any more hurt. Hasn't it been through enough?

"I don't think you're messing with me, but . . ." Do I dare say what I'm thinking?

"But what?" He gently grips my chin, locking his gaze with mine. "I'm listening. I want to hear everything you want to share."

"What if you end up breaking my heart anyway?"

He squeezes his eyes shut then opens them, determination shining through. "I'll make mistakes. I'll sometimes fail your expectations. But you have to know, Simone, you have my heart. I know we haven't known each other very long, but my heart is yours."

My mouth dries at his proclamation. Is he saying . . .

"I'm falling in love with you."

"How?" My voice sounds breathless.

"How could I not? You're everything I never knew I needed. I can't help but believe God led me to Anchor Cove just to meet you and Taj."

Tears spill over before I'm even aware I'm crying. My heart is full to bursting, but honestly, the fear is still high as well. Derrick's words are amazing. I'll remember them for the rest of my life. Yet my brain keeps shouting: *How can this work? How will we stay together?*

"I know you're worried about the future, and I've been in the same boat. Actually, I was until a couple of weeks ago when God showed me I needed to trust Him in every single detail in my life."

"I trust Him." Instead of the words coming out assured, there's a hesitancy that surprises me. Don't I trust the Lord? I've said repeatedly how much He's been my rock and the reason I've been provided for at every stage of life. Looking back on my life, I clearly see His handiwork.

Yet the more I dissect the fear in my heart and stare at the assurance in Derrick's eyes, the more I realize I don't trust the Lord as much as I believe I do.

"Help my unbelief," I whisper.

Derrick cups my face. "He's got us, Simone. Whatever His plan is for our lives. Wherever He guides us, it's for our good. We can rest in that because *He's* good." He leans forward and places a kiss on my forehead.

I'm realizing this is his signature move to reassure me and connect with me physically as well. I hold on to Derrick's wrist as he rests his lips against my head. I don't want this moment to end. I don't want this comfort or feeling of security to abate.

However, I definitely need to pray that I let go of the fear and grasp on to the hope God is offering me. I want to trust in Him because He's a God that doesn't break promises. If He says He's for me, then He is. It's as simple as that, and as complex to live out.

Chapter Twenty-Two

Derrick

August is here before I'm ready for it. What once would've given me anxiety is now simply an acknowledgment of facts. In a month, I'll return to Virginia to live with my mother if I don't have a different plan in place. I haven't asked the Lord for an update since that revelation last month where He made it clear He'd give me directions in His own time.

My run this morning isn't one filled with worry. I'm actually able to enjoy the scenery as the sun rises above the ocean. There aren't a lot of people out at six in the morning, but there is a couple or two watching the sunrise as well as a dog walker. The fresh air calms me in a way the run doesn't. My knees may want me to find a different way to keep in shape, but my body needs the endorphins that will improve my mood later on.

I jog up the steps to my rental, ready for a shower and breakfast, in that order. Simone won't be up until around eight and Taj sleeps in a little longer unless the youth group has some activity planned. I love that the church ensures the kids enjoy their summer but also that they won't waste time away. They'll be doing volunteer work all next week to help the city and experiencing why being a servant matters to the Lord. Pastor David already asked me to participate. I agreed for two reasons. One, it's been a while since I was active in church. I never had an opportunity to volunteer at one in the past since my deployment schedule pulled me away and I didn't want to disappoint anyone if I couldn't do what I said I would. Two, I really enjoyed my time with the kids on our camping trip.

The morning goes by quietly so when my cell phone rings, I jump at the sudden noise. Torres is calling again.

"Hey, man, how's it going?"

"Benjamin, my brother, I've got a job for you."

My brow wrinkles in confusion. Torres works for Uncle Sam. How can he offer me a job? "Come again?"

"Well, not me per se, but I know people. My brother-in-law's company needs a manager. They offer a decent wage—definitely better than military pay. Benefits and PTO are available as well."

"Okay. What's the catch?" Try as I might, I can't recall where Torres's brother-in-law lives. Torres is from Houston, Texas, but there's something niggling at the back of my mind suggesting that's not where his sister lives.

"Catch is they need someone to start in two weeks."

My mouth drops. "Oh."

"Yeah. Not sure how your summer romance has progressed and if you'd be amenable to that."

"Where are they? Not in Houston, right?"

"Oh no. My sister and her family live out in DC."

That's about three hours from Anchor Cove. Is that too far to commute from here during the week? Or could I get a place in DC and come to Anchor Cove on the weekends until Simone and I figure out the rest of the details?

"What's the salary?"

Torres names a figure that nearly has my eyes bugging out. Then again, the East Coast is more expensive than other places.

"What do you think?" he asks.

"I'm going to need to pray about it. When do you need an answer by?"

"Well, Vega, my brother-in-law, would like to interview you. It's more of a formality, but he'll discuss everything and let you know when he needs a decision by."

"All right. Should I call him?"

"Nah. If you give me permission to pass on your number, he'll handle the rest."

"Sure. I appreciate you thinking of me, man."

"Anytime, bro. Keep me posted."

A few hours later, I'm wearing my best-looking button-down shirt and doing a virtual interview with Vega Rivera.

"I appreciate you being flexible in meeting so soon. I've had the chance to look over your resume and it's quite impressive."

"Thank you."

Mr. Rivera asks the standard interview questions then he opens the floor to me. "Do you have any questions?"

"Yes. How many people would I be managing?"

"We'd have you working at our DC office, which has about fifty people there." He goes on to explain their structure and all they would need from me. "There's a chance for promotion and to transfer to any of our offices as long as we can fill your current position. We have an office in northern Virginia, southern Maryland, and we're looking at moving down to the Florida panhandle sometime next year." He goes on to explain the benefits and the salary, which is more than Torres quoted. "How does that all sound?"

"Pretty great."

He flashes a smile. "Torres said you'd need time to think about it because you're in Anchor Cove right now on vacation."

"Right. I've met someone local, and I need to talk this over with her."

"I see. Is it serious? Not asking in an official capacity." He chuckles.

"It is. Torres has been giving me dating advice."

Rivera rolls his eyes. "Dude is as single as they come. But he does give good advice despite that."

I laugh. "He's annoyingly good at it."

"Well, if you could let me know in a few days, that would be great. I have some other possibilities, but you'd make a better choice."

I dip my head in acknowledgement. I'm relieved to finally have a job offer. "Thanks for your time."

"Likewise. Hope to hear from you soon."

I disconnect the video feed and stare out into space.

Is this what's next, Lord? Is this the answer You've prepared beforehand or just something the world's trying to distract me with?

Nothing feels settled or confirmed. I pray God guides me in my conversation with Simone. I'm not sure how she'll react, knowing this job is so close yet still so far away. Is the commute for this job even sustainable? I'm not sure, but I do have hope everything will work out.

My doorbell rings and my shoulders tense before I purposely take a breath and lower them back down. It's probably Simone. And as nervous as that makes me, I have to remember that God's guiding us. If He wants me to take this job, He'll make it known.

Simone

Derrick fills the gap between the doorframe, and my heart lightens at the sight of him.

"Morning." I smile.

He snakes an arm around my waist and pulls me close. "Hey, you." He nuzzles the curve of my neck and my insides melt.

I wind my arms around his neck and kiss his cheek in a, *hello. I missed you. I'm so glad to see you again.* Dating him makes me so sappy, but I don't care.

Our nuzzles soon cease as our lips find their way to each other. He pulls me inside the house, closing the door behind me, and then my back is against the door as the kiss takes on a different tone. One that's warm and unhurried, with a freedom that we can explore each other in this way. Just when I think the sweetness of the kiss will overwhelm me, Derrick pulls away and leans his forehead against mine.

"Best 'good morning' ever."

A raspy laugh leaves my lips as my voice tries to find its normal tone and not the *I'm falling faster than I can keep up* way.

"I can make this happen every morning if Anchor Cove is on the table."

He sighs and puts space between us. "About that..."

No, no, no. I straighten, folding my arms across my chest. "I don't like the sound of that."

"It's not all bad." He gently tugs at my arm until I drop it for him, then he interlaces our fingers and guides us to the sofa.

When he pulls me down to sit next to him, there's no space between us. He wraps his arm around my shoulder and tucks me close. I sigh and rest my head against his chest.

"Fine. Tell me how much chocolate I'll need."

He laughs. "Hear me out first, 'kay?"

I nod against his chest, and when he starts to speak the timbre of his voice vibrates against me, soothing me in a way I didn't know I needed.

"An old friend called to let me know his brother-in-law is hiring."

"Where at?"

"DC."

I bite my lip, considering the distance between here and there.

"I haven't accepted the offer. He knows I need to talk it over with someone special."

"Did you really say that?"

"Yes."

The fact that he thought of me first has me wrapping my arms around his waist and squeezing tight. I loosen my grip but continue resting my hand against his middle as he finishes telling me about the job.

"What does that mean for us?"

"Well, if I take it, there's a couple of things that could happen."

"Like?"

"I could rent a place in Anchor Cove and commute every day."

"No." I wince. "Sorry for interrupting, but that's a three-hour drive. Say you work nine to five. That's extending an eight-hour day to fourteen. You'd be exhausted. You'll get back home to fall into bed only to turn around and do it all over again."

"But I'd have an hour to hang out with you before I fall asleep."

"No. Next option."

His huff of laughter has my body moving up then down against his chest. "Other option is to get a place in DC. Then on Friday, drive up here and spend the weekend with you and Taj before I return back to DC on Sunday evening."

"More sustainable, but for how long?"

"Until Taj graduates? Then maybe we'd marry, then you move to DC with me."

His statement is said calmly, but I hear the vulnerability in his voice. We haven't talked about marriage so concretely before, even though he expressed that it's his end goal.

I sit up in order to look into his eyes. "You'd do that drive every weekend for the next three years?"

"To see you? Yes."

"What about me? What if I want to come see you?"

He smiles, smoothing a curl back from my face. "I'd love it if you came to visit me."

"Does that mean this is what we're choosing?"

"No."

Relief floods me, but I still myself. Just because he's saying *no* doesn't mean the answer will remain that way. "How come? Isn't this the answer to your prayers?"

"I don't know. I don't want to jump the gun just because I was desperate for some answers a short while ago. Who knows? God could have something better for us."

"Us?" I can't stop the smile on my face.

Judging from the corresponding grin on Derrick's, he likes the idea of an *us* as much as I do.

"Us." He kisses me softly, once, twice, and a third time.

Before I get too wrapped up in the affection, Derrick slides a finger down my cheek. "Should we pray together about the job?"

I nod, too pleased he's keeping the *us* in prayer as well. He prays for the Lord's guidance and for Him to give us ears to hear. And I admit, in the midst of his sweet prayer, I open my eyes to watch him. This is something I never saw growing up. Though my parents didn't argue with each other, I didn't really see them act *together*. Their relationship always seemed more duty than love.

Over the years, I've heard of how married women pray with their husbands, but I haven't been privy to what that looks like. If it resembles anything like what Derrick is showing me, then I understand why married women always get that soft expression on their face when they talk about their spouse.

Derrick starts ending the prayer, so I close my eyes once more and say "amen" at the end. I loop my arms around his neck and drop a quick kiss on his lips.

"Thank you."

"For what?"

"For being you."

He draws me closer and holds me. No kisses. No words. Just an embrace that speaks louder than any thank-you ever could.

Chapter Twenty-Three

Derrick

The majority of my time in Anchor Cove has been spent griping about how I didn't know what was going to happen next in my career. Not that my fears weren't valid. However, standing in the church listening to instructions on how to assemble packets for the homeless brings a much-needed perspective.

I have some savings that will last me a while. I have a job offer. I have a roof over my head and clothes on my back. In fact, I know where my next meal is coming from—the church, because they're feeding all of us volunteers today. However, the people we're creating these packets of toiletries and food for don't even have those basic necessities.

It's humbling.

"Have you done this before?" I ask Taj once we've been assigned stations in the assembly line.

He'll be adding hand sanitizer to the packs while I'm in charge of travel-size tissues.

"No, this is my first time." He glances at me. "Surreal, huh?"

"It's heartbreaking to think that others don't have the basic needs, right?"

"Yeah. It feels like this isn't enough."

"Maybe not, but it's a start."

Tommy passes a plastic bag to me. I add a pack of tissues before handing it to Taj.

"Have you volunteered in other ways before this?" Taj asks.

"Yeah, in the military. They give you plenty of opportunities to volunteer in various places. I've volunteered for Meals on Wheels and even at some sporting events."

"Wow. Did you volunteer because God wants us to serve others or for some other reason?"

"Doing Meals on Wheels was to serve others. The sporting events was because I was hoping to see someone famous," I quip. "But now that I'm retired, I hope to do more things to help others."

"I think I'd like to do that too."

We're quiet for a few minutes as everyone works to fill each gallon-size Ziploc with toiletries. The food assembly line will be after we finish with all the items dedicated to these bags.

"D?"

"Hm?"

"Have you heard anything on the job front?" A furrow creases the center of Taj's brow, showing how much he cares about my answer.

"I actually heard something last week."

His mouth drops, and the hand sanitizer he's holding falls onto the table. He blinks, picks it up, and goes back to passing the plastic bag to the next person. "How come you didn't say anything?"

"Well, I did talk to your mother, and we agreed to pray.

When I went to turn down the job because I didn't feel like God had given me an answer yet, the guy gave me more time to think about it."

Taj glances away but not before I notice a flash of hurt. And then it hits me: I didn't ask his opinion. I've been intentional in showing he matters, but I forgot to bring the job offer up to him.

"I'm sorry." I move closer to him, placing a hand on his shoulder. "I wasn't trying to leave you out."

"But you did." He jerks his shoulder away.

I swallow. "I'm sorry. I'll make sure not to do it again."

He nods.

I move back to my spot as we continue filling bags. After a few more seconds, I peek at him. "Can I get your opinion on the offer?"

"Took you long enough."

I chuckle, then tell Taj about where the job is and the commute option that Simone shot down—which Taj does as well. A look of consternation fills his face when I share about the option of visiting each weekend until he graduates. Something I've said upset him, but I'm not exactly sure what.

"What's wrong?" I ask.

Taj looks away and angrily drops a hand sanitizer into the next Ziploc before thrusting it at the teen to his left. "You'll just go back and forth for the next three years?"

"Your mom doesn't want to leave Anchor Cove, Taj. You're still in high school. Y'all have friends and family here, a community."

"But we wouldn't have you. Not full-time anyway."

His words stun me. There's no other explanation for the wonder drumming through me or the humility at hearing he'd rather have me around than be close to the people he's known his whole life. Granted, he doesn't use those exact words, but the sentiment is the same.

"Taj . . ." I'm overcome and can't seem to gather my thoughts.

"I look up to you, D. You're not just my mom's boyfriend. You know, if you ever married her, you'd be . . ." He clears his throat. "I mean, you would be like, my um—" He licks his lips, nerves suddenly making words difficult.

"Your stepdad?" I say quietly.

He nods jerkily, like the word has bigger ramifications than he wants to admit. Ramifications I've thought of but am just now seeing how big of an impact it would truly be.

"Have you told your mom what that means to you?"

"No," he croaks. He clears his throat, facing forward, away from my eyes.

I do the same, understanding he needs to speak without me watching his every move.

"I never thought she'd choose to be anywhere but where you are," Taj mutters.

"I appreciate the thought, but you come first to her."

He sighs. "But when she marries, shouldn't her husband come first? Isn't that biblical?"

Oh boy. This is a can of worms I don't want to touch. At least not without talking to Simone first. "Maybe this is a conversation we need to have together with your mom."

Taj groans as if he can't wait that long. "Fine. If we have to wait until dinner, then fine."

"It's fine?" I glance at him.

He cracks a grin and shakes his head. Now that I know how Taj feels, it really does seem like everything will be okay. I'm not sure how Simone will handle this new development, but I'm a firm believer if we continuously check in with one another, it'll be a lot smoother than if we all keep our thoughts to ourselves.

Simone

Taj keeps side-eyeing Derrick as if waiting for him to introduce an important conversation. At first, I couldn't figure out why he was looking at Derrick. Then when I caught Derrick's subtle shake of the head, I realized they were both in on whatever the topic is. Now that I'm placing tonight's dessert on the table, I've had enough of the secretive glances.

"Out with it, you two."

"Mom, how come you didn't tell me Derrick got a job offer?"

I plop down in the chair. "What do you mean?"

"I mean, Derrick knows me and you are a package deal, right?"

"I do," Derrick says.

Now I'm thinking of those words but in a different context. I barely wipe the stars from my eyes before Taj continues.

"If we're a package deal, shouldn't I get a say in what happens to us in the future? On whether or not he takes this new job?"

Uh . . . "Well, Derrick and I prayed. He agreed to decline the offer because he didn't think there was enough time to really discern what God was saying."

"Right. He told me that." My son leans forward. "But when the guy offered him more thinking time, wouldn't that have been a good day to loop me in? Ask me what I think?"

"Taj, this impacts Derrick the most. He's the one who needs a job."

"Nuh-uh. Not buying it. You want to be with Derrick. *I* want Derrick as a stepfather."

My heart palpitates—or perhaps it actually stops, because I'm in a fog and may need to be resuscitated. "What did you say?" I whisper.

"Mom, Derrick is awesome. I want the chance to see what it's like to have a dad around. I don't want him visiting us on the weekends until I graduate high school, because then that means I'll go off to college and not know what it's like to have a dad around the house twenty-four-seven. One who yells at me to put on deodorant like you do but understands I'm going to stink because he was outside shooting hoops with me, ya know?"

Derrick reaches across the table, linking our fingers together. Obviously, he knows I need an anchor because hearing my son pour out his heart before me *and* before the man in question has me needing a moment to process my emotions.

"I'm . . . I'm a little surprised."

"Why?"

"I hoped you liked Derrick. I guess it never occurred to me you were thinking all of these things." But shouldn't it have? Was I shortsighted?

I wanted to make sure that my heart wouldn't get broken, and I even remembered to pray that Taj's heart would be cared for as well. Apparently, I never considered what Taj was actually looking forward to.

"Well, now you know. I don't want Derrick commuting three hours one-way every day. I don't want him to live away from us until I graduate high school." Taj leans back, as if all his energy is finally spent.

"Then what *do* you want, son?" I stare at him. The boy who's morphing into a man right before my very eyes.

One guess as to who has influenced Taj to start speaking his mind. It's one of those changes I've been noticing since my son started spending so much time with Derrick.

"I want to be a family. And I honestly don't care whether we have a Maryland zip code or a Washington, DC one."

I nod, because what else can I do? I'm not sure moving from Anchor Cove is so easy for me to agree to. Not that I don't want to be with Derrick, but I had it in my head this is where Taj and I had built our life. This is where all of my properties are. How could I discount all of that and follow a man I've only known for two and a half months?

Taj stands and looks at the both of us before staring back at me. "Don't leave me out, 'kay?"

"Promise." I reach over and squeeze his hand before he trudges down the hall to his room. "Wow," I say.

"Hope that didn't feel like an ambush."

"It didn't." I shake my head. "I knew y'all wanted to talk about something, but I didn't realize Taj had all of those . . . thoughts."

Derrick chuckles as he rubs the back of his neck. "Same. He corrected me at church today for not including him in the original discussion."

"He was hurt?"

Derrick nods.

I close my eyes and drop my head into my hands. "Being a parent is so hard."

"I see that. But Simone, don't forget you're doing a wonderful job. He's such a good kid, and that's a reflection of you."

I sniff. "But I made him feel like he didn't matter."

"And you promised you wouldn't do it again. That's what

he'll remember. And when we have to make another decision, we'll include him."

"You're right." I let out a small sigh. "Do you think you should take the job? Should we all move to DC?"

An uneasy expression crosses his face. "I'm still not convinced that's the answer. And I know how much you want to be here."

"Taj has a point though. The thought of waiting three years sounds awful. I was happy when you turned him down. Now that Taj is pointing out we could all move, I wonder if that's the obvious answer. Going with you, I mean. It's not like we can't come back to Anchor Cove at some point in time." I could get someone to run my properties, right?

"True."

My phone rings and I flinch at the *Unknown* that flashes across the screen.

Derrick notices. "Do you know who that is?"

"I think so."

His brows raise, waiting on my answer.

"My mother."

"Your mother?" he splutters.

"She called when you guys went camping. She tried to ask for forgiveness, but I . . ." I squeeze the sides of my head. "I just can't."

"Simone, sweetheart, why didn't you say anything?"

At the endearment, my eyes water and I fall into his arms. "I don't know," I mumble, holding on to him tightly.

Derrick rubs soothing circles on my back, and we stay like that long after the phone stops buzzing. When I sit back into my chair and he meets my gaze, I realize there are some things I'll have to resolve tonight. Might as well be the topic of my mother and the reason forgiving her seems impossible.

"She kicked me out of the house, Derrick."

"I know, beautiful. That had to have hurt so much."

"And now she wants me to forgive just because she called to apologize after fifteen years of silence?"

"The forgiveness isn't for her."

"I know that here." I point to the side of my head. "But here . . ." I place my finger against my chest where my heart is aching at the mere thought of forgiving my mother. "I don't want to do it."

"If you don't and she keeps calling, how will that affect you?"

I sigh. "I'm going to feel more guilty than I already do."

"Okay." He nods slowly. "And if you do forgive her, what does that look like to you?"

Hmm. That's actually a good question. No one said forgiveness equals reconciliation. At this point, my mom hasn't done anything to earn a restored relationship. "Maybe it looks like me not feeling guilty?"

Derrick smiles and leans forward, brushing a kiss across my cheek. When he pulls back to gaze into my eyes, it's with sympathy and understanding. "Forgiveness is for you. Not her. And it's on your timetable. God will help you, if that's what you want. But He also won't force you."

"You're right."

"But?"

"But nothing. You're right."

He chuckles at that, and I wrap my arms around him. "Thank you for listening."

"Anytime, beautiful. Anytime."

Chapter Twenty-Four

Derrick

With a final swipe of the roller, I finish painting the hallway leading to the teaching rooms at the church. The church looks brighter, and I'm glad I could do something to contribute to the place that's made me feel at home. I put the lid on the empty paint can and start gathering my supplies.

"Hey, Derrick. All done?" Pastor David wanders down the hall, hands in his short pockets.

"Yep. What do you think?"

He looks around. "Fantastic. The place looks so much brighter."

"I had the same thought."

He holds out a hand, and I shift the supplies to shake it. "Thanks again for doing this for us."

"Of course. Happy to help."

"Hey, do you have a moment before you go?"

I stare at the stuff in my hand, then set it down on the ground. I'm not sure how long this conversation is going to last. "Sure. Everything okay?"

"Yes, yes. Nothing's wrong. It just so happens we had a board meeting earlier."

I nod, wondering what this has to do with me.

"Some of the board members were also chaperones on the camping trip. You remember Tommy?"

"I do."

"Right, so he's a church board member. Anyway," Pastor David waves a hand in the air as if he can tell he's rambling and not connecting the dots fast enough for me, "we got to talking and the suggestion came up to accelerate our plan for expanding the youth ministry to now. It's been on our wish list for a while, but life has kept it on the back burner. We've prayed and we all believed God is saying now's the time."

"Wow. Sounds great." I'm sure Taj will appreciate any expansions they make to the ministry.

Pastor David chuckles. "Guess I'm taking the long-winded route. Basically, we'd like to bring you on as the new youth director. You'd be in charge of developing a program that will continue to grow our youth in discipleship as they seek a relationship with God. You'd lead things like the camping trip and any other events that you come up with and the pastoral staff agree upon."

I recognize every word he's saying but it sounds too . . . too . . . *perfect?*

"But I'm not a pastor. I've never been to seminary and, I mean . . ." I scratch the back of my head. "How do you even consider me qualified for such a position?"

"Well, Derrick, everyone on staff agreed you were the best man for the job. We saw how easily you connected with the youth on the camping trip. There was an easy camaraderie between you and the teens when we put together the care kits as well. The wisdom you've shared every time you've interacted with the youth has been biblically sound, and you haven't missed a Sunday church attendance yet. I also heard you tell the boys how much you value time in the Word and prayer with God. You obviously have a good foundation in the Lord."

I nod, though I think it's more out of instinct than actual understanding. "And that's good enough?"

"We believe God is calling you, so *His* desire is all we need. Still, we want you to pray about it. Don't say no just because you feel unequipped. But we're also happy to fund some schooling if you wish to seek a seminary degree. It's not required to be the youth director, but it's an option if you wish."

My heart is hammering so hard I think I might need to sit for a minute. This feeling coursing through me tells me I'm a lot more interested than I expected to be. It's like my heart is tugging me one way despite my brain trying to go in the opposite direction.

"I'll definitely go home and pray about it."

He claps me on the back. "Good. Let me know when the Lord answers you. I have no doubt He will."

"Thanks, Pastor David."

He grins, eyes crinkling. "David is just fine."

This isn't the first time he's said that, but I still feel a little uneasy dropping the title. Twenty years in the service, plus a childhood background of calling every minister *pastor* means it's not going to be so easy to adjust. But if I were to work with him, maybe I'd finally get to the point of calling him by his first name.

"I'm sure there's also a certain person you'll be talking this over with."

Now I'm the one with a smile on my face. "Two people. I have to talk with the both of them."

"I knew you were a smart man." He turns to walk back to where he came from. "Have a good afternoon."

"You too."

I stare unseeingly for a moment then jolt into action. There will be conversations, but I'm actually really eager to talk to the Lord about this. Could this be what He's had for me all along? I've never imagined a life in ministry. Though I love God, studying the Word, and talking with others about the truths we find in Scripture, it never translated to ministry work for me.

I'm practically bursting at the seams at the idea that this could be my future. Should I go to seminary if I take the job? Can I learn a new vocation, go back to school, and be in a new relationship all at once? It sounds like a lot, but when I think of Simone and Taj, wholly worth it. If I accept this job, I don't have to move. If I say yes, Simone and Taj won't have to move either. Honestly, that's more appealing than anything.

Yes, Taj offered to leave his friends behind, but the idea doesn't sit right with me. Their whole support system is here, and I'm just one guy. It's so much easier for me to come here than to uproot their whole lives.

The more I think about the details, the more this feels like God's leading. And the more I believe this is from God, the happier I get. I can't imagine Simone and Taj's faces when I bring this up, but I sure can't wait to see their reactions.

As soon as I'm done cleaning up after myself, I walk toward my rental house. Time to be alone with the Lord before I stop by and see the two people who will probably be more thrilled than I currently am.

Simone

Tonight, we're going to Amy's house for a seafood broil. Now that the stomach bug is a thing of the past and she's entered her second trimester, she wants to get to know Derrick better. Or rather, Amy and Chris want to grill my boyfriend. But I don't care. Derrick can handle whatever they throw at him.

I sigh, the kind that sounds completely lovesick, but I really don't care. I've waited a long time for this kind of romance, and I'm savoring every moment.

"Mom, have you seen my Goku shirt?"

"Yes. It's in the dryer because you didn't fold your clothes."

"Bruh." Taj trudges toward the laundry room. "Why didn't you bring my clothes to my room?"

"Excuse me?"

He freezes then swings to face me. "I'm sorry. I meant no disrespect."

"I guess you forgot who does your laundry?" I fold my arms across my chest. Even though I'm chilling on the couch waiting for Derrick to come by, I still make sure I look imposing.

"No. I do."

"Then why didn't your clothes make it to your room?"

"Because it's my fault."

"Thank you." I beam at him, and he resists the urge to roll his eyes or mumble.

Instead, my son quietly leaves the living room, and a couple of minutes later he returns with a basket of clean laundry.

The doorbell rings, and I jump off the couch, flinging the door open without even trying to play it cool. And what do I find? My boyfriend leaning against the doorjamb, looking too good in a T-shirt and shorts.

He pulls me into his arms and kisses me hello in the best of ways. I sigh, curling my arms around his neck and melting into the kiss. Finally, we pull apart and I blink, trying to get my bearings. "Will you greet me like that every time?"

"If you want," he says in a husky tone.

"I want."

He kisses me softly on the lips. "Then you got it."

I take his hand and we walk to the couch. Derrick sits first, and I curl up next to his side as he places an arm around my shoulders.

"You ready for the craziness that is the Miller household?"

"Sure. I haven't met Chris yet."

"You'll love them. They're the best."

Taj comes back into the living room. "Hey, D."

Derrick sits up and he and Taj exchange a complicated dap that makes my eyes almost cross. "I'm glad you came in here. I wanted to talk to you and your mom."

Taj sits on the ottoman, facing us. "What's up? Everything okay? Is this about the DC job?"

"Taj, give him a chance to answer," I interject before my son can come up with more questions.

Derrick chuckles. "Yeah, it's about the DC job, sort of."

"Sort of?" I shift out of his embrace to watch him. "What do you mean?"

"I got another job offer."

"Another one?" Taj's jaw drops open. "A good one? Better pay? Where is it?"

I send a *hush up* look to Taj.

"Sorry," he mumbles.

"It's okay. But how about I tell you about the job and then

you can ask all your questions when I'm done?" Derrick looks at me. "You too," he whispers.

"We're listening." Taj props his chin on his hands, an intent expression on his face.

"Pastor David offered me a job at the church working as the youth director." At our silence, Derrick continues. "It's not as much money as the job in DC. However, y'all wouldn't have to move. I could be here all the time. Plus, I get a monthly retirement check from the military so if I spend my money wisely, we'll be okay."

"Don't forget Mom has all her rental properties." Taj winks at me.

I have to stifle my laugh because while I appreciate him bringing that up, my mind is whirling at the fact Pastor David offered Derrick a job.

Yes! This is what we've been waiting for. Praying for.

Derrick will want to pray about this decision, but I already feel the answer down to my marrow. This is such a God move. We think we have it all figured out, then boom, He drops the perfect job in our laps. One that will allow Derrick and me to continue to grow closer together.

"What do y'all think?" Derrick asks.

"I say yes." Taj starts first. "Anchor Cove is the best and we need a real youth program, not something that's an afterthought."

He's right. The church is serving more and more teens and if Derrick can help guide them in their faith journey, I think it will be a beautiful thing.

"Any objections?" Derrick asks Taj.

"Nope." He stands. "Since you know my opinion, I'm going to head to my room. Misha wanted to chat, and I told her I'd call her before we left tonight."

"Go ahead," I say, though he really wasn't asking my permission.

Still, Taj nods and walks out of the room.

I curl back against Derrick's side. "How do you feel about the offer?"

"I'm in awe of how God works." He tells me about the offer for seminary classes. Shares how he prayed and the direction he thought God was leading. "What do you think about it all?"

"I think it's a yes. I feel it right here." I point to the center of my chest.

Derrick leans his forehead against mine. "I'm so relieved," he murmurs.

"Me too." I cup his face. "You in Anchor Cove full-time is a dream come true."

"Now I have the rest of the summer to find a place to stay."

"What? Why?"

"Simone, you realize I'm just renting for the summer. When the calendar shows Labor Day, I'm out and your next renter is in."

Okay, so he has a point, but also . . . "Your girlfriend owns many rental properties. Why can't you just switch to one of those until you one day live with her?" My eyes widen as I recognize how that sounds. "I mean—"

He chuckles and places a finger across my lips. "You mean after we're married."

I nod.

"Okay. Which rental do you have open that's comparable in price?"

"After Labor Day, all my rentals go down in price because the tourist season is over. But don't worry, I'll give you a boyfriend discount as well."

Derrick's eyes light up, and the happiness shining from them sparks me from the inside out. "Boyfriend discount?"

"Yes, exactly."

"The only thing left I'll have to do is drive to my mom's to get my stuff. That's where I had the military ship everything when I retired."

"*We* can drive there together."

He sighs contentedly. "I like this *we* stuff."

"So do I, boyfriend. So do I."

Chapter Twenty-Five

Derrick

I FLIP THE BURGERS THEN LOOK UP FROM THE GRILL. Simone's laughing with Amy as they chat. Simone's practically glowing with happiness. Now that I have a plan, have a job, *and* a place to stay, she's overjoyed. Amy's starting to show, and it makes me wonder if Simone and I will ever have a little one of our own. That's something to talk about at some point in the future.

My gaze finds Taj. He's doing a bean bag toss with his friends. Misha's gazing at him adoringly. Do I need to start having a conversation about dating and the way to do it God's way? I make a mental note to talk it over with Simone. She's not ready to see her son grow up, but I don't think it'll be long before he's thinking of dating. Probably already has.

Chris walks over to me and nods. "Hey, man. Need any help?"

"Nah, I'm good." I point to his boys. "They want hot dogs, right?"

"Right, but barely grilled." He rolls his eyes. "I've never met pickier kids."

"Think your next one will be a boy too?"

"I can't decide if another boy will be easier since we're already used to boys, or if I should beg for mercy on behalf of my wife and ask for a girl."

I laugh. "Do you really want her surrounded by four men?"

He stares at her lovingly. "If anyone can handle it, it's Amy. But she deserves the world, so I guess I'll start praying for a girl."

Since Amy started feeling better from her morning sickness, Simone and I have hung out with her and Chris a lot. My girlfriend was right. They're a fun couple. I've also managed to wrangle Chris to come to some of the youth events, reminding him Billy and Jimmy will be in that age group before he can blink. But honestly, it's more because he's got a lot of wisdom he hides under jokes and that works with the teens better than anything else.

This month, I'll start my first two seminary classes. I signed up for a correspondence program that only requires me to attend in person one week a semester. I'm looking forward to becoming better equipped for the new call God's placed on my life. I never imagined everything I could ever want would be waiting for me in this beach town, but I'm so glad that I didn't try and plan my way to here. Learning to trust God and trust His plans for me was an important part of the journey. There's no way I could've orchestrated how everything fell into place the way it did.

Chris and I chat a little more. When the burgers are done, I fill a foil pan with the grilled meat and bring the food to the table Simone sat up in the backyard.

A shuffling sounds behind me, and I pivot around to see a woman walk cautiously into the backyard. My chest tightens as I realize exactly who she is. She looks exactly how I picture Simone in about thirty more years.

I move forward and extend my hand. "Hi, Mrs. Avery. I'm Derrick Benjamin, Simone's boyfriend."

She smiles. "It's nice to meet you." She looks around the yard and freezes when she spies her daughter. "Do you think she really wants me here?" Her voice comes out quiet and hesitant.

"I do. Plus, your grandson is looking forward to getting to know you."

Her hands wring together as if she's not buying my reassurance.

Simone finally called her mother back and they've been talking these past couple of weeks. When we decided to throw a Labor Day party before Taj starts school, I encouraged her to reach out to her mom as an olive branch. Simone's nervous about reuniting with her mother, especially knowing that her father still would rather maintain his distance.

"Would you like me to call her over?"

Mrs. Avery nods slowly. "Please."

I turn, hoping to catch Simone's eye without yelling across the backyard. As if sensing my gaze, she turns her head my way and smiles at me. I barely keep my sigh of relief in check. Instead, I motion for her to come over. A quizzical expression pops on her face, but whatever answers in mine has her straightening and walking quickly to my side.

When I step aside so she can see her mother, she immediately reaches for my hand. I press the other to the small of her back, letting her know I'm right here. I've got her and she can do this.

"Mom . . ."

Mrs. Avery's eyes fill up. "Simone, baby." She sniffs. "You're so beautiful. Can I . . . can I hug you?"

Simone nods and Mrs. Avery wraps her daughter up in

her arms. They're both crying as I step back to give them a private moment.

Lord God, please let this heal some wounds and be the beginning of something beautiful.

Simone

I don't actually remember the last time my mom hugged me, but this embrace right here is undoing me in so many ways. Since her first phone call, I've prayed and begged God to help me truly forgive her. I don't want a single root of bitterness or unforgiveness in my heart. And judging by the flow of tears free-falling right now, God has done the work I prayed for. I'm lighter than I have been in years and so thankful that I can hug her without any ill thought toward her *or* my father.

Knowing my dad still doesn't want to see me stung at first, but then I realized that his stance hasn't changed at all. He can't do me any more harm to me since he hasn't been in my life all these years later. Staying angry at him just hurts me, and I'm so ready for a new phase of life. Which means even though he's not here asking for my forgiveness like my mother is, he has it. If he wants to see me one day, I'll be open to it, and if he doesn't, I won't be crushed.

He doesn't determine my worth. Only the Lord Jesus has that power.

Mom lets go of me, and I wipe at my face. Before I can search for a napkin, Derrick hands me a box of tissues. I'm not sure where he went to find these, but I'm thankful he anticipated this. My mom plucks a bunch, and we mop up our faces.

"Thank you for inviting me," she says with a tremulous smile.

"You're welcome. Would you like to meet your grandson?"

Her eyes water again, and she nods. "I would love to."

Derrick calls for Taj to come over, and I watch as he jogs toward Derrick. Since Derrick accepted the youth director job, we've all been so happy. He's over every day to eat with us and he and Taj go off and do their own thing at times. I love the relationship that's developing between them. I can't wait for the day when I'll call myself Mrs. Benjamin and Taj can call Derrick *Dad*.

Taj slows down, and when he sees my mom, he does a double take.

"Whoa. It's like seeing twins." He shows a mouth full of teeth. "You must be my grandma."

"Mom, meet your grandson, Taj Samuel Avery. He's fifteen, five-five, and a hundred and twenty pounds."

We all laugh as I give stats as if he were a newborn.

"Taj, meet your grandma, Dawn Avery."

"I'm a hugger. Are you?"

"For family." He steps forward and embraces her.

I place a hand on my heart, trying to keep calm. I never thought I'd see this day, and now that it's come, I'm so thankful.

Once introductions are made, everyone else fills up their plates and finds spots to eat. We brought a few tables out here and I recently added a fire pit at Taj's suggestion. He liked the idea of having our own family campfire discussions like they did on the youth trip. Once the sun goes down, we'll light it and bring out the stuff to make s'mores.

Lord God, thank You so much for the many ways You've blessed me.

When I look around the tables and see all of our friends *and* family, my heart wants to burst. Back when the summer first started, I never thought that God would answer my prayer about what happens after Taj leaves for college in such a way. Or if my loneliness would ever go away.

God is so good.

Thank You for seeing me and hearing me, Father. I love You so much and am so thankful to You.

Epilogue

Simone

"Mom, I can't find my cap and gown." Taj rubs the back of his head as he paces back and forth in a button-down shirt, tie, and slacks. My little boy is a man now.

"I steamed the gown and hung both in the laundry room."

He takes off racing toward the room and comes back holding the cap in hand and the gown by the hanger. "Thanks. Dad's still driving me, right?"

I nod, praying that Abigail stays asleep. She just finished nursing and she's knocked out. At six months, my baby girl is the most precious sight I've seen since I held my firstborn eighteen years ago.

"See you at the ceremony." He waves and heads for the garage.

I sigh, trying to keep the tears at bay. *Today is a good day. You're not losing him. Life is just changing.*

Once Derrick moved to Anchor Cove full-time, we dated until he proposed on New Year's Eve, and we rang in the new year as an engaged couple and married in April. Our spring wedding was beautiful. A little chilly by the beach but worth the ambiance.

I'd been surprised to get pregnant the following February but the two men in my life were so excited. Though I'd been worried Taj would feel annoyed that his mom was pregnant when he was a teen, he took it in stride. He loves Abby so much and helps around the house when he can. He's been accepted to George Mason, a college in northern Virginia, so he's promised to come back on the weekends to spend time with the three of us.

I shift to stand, still holding on to my little one and head down the hall to her nursery. While she naps, I'll shower and get ready for the graduation ceremony. Amy and crew will be joining us. She had a little girl almost two years ago and is due to have a second daughter any day now. She claims this is the last child, but I catch the expression on her face every time she watches her kids. She loves them so much, I won't be surprised if the Millers keep expanding their family.

My mom is also joining the graduation festivities. Our relationship is in a much better place right now. Taj loves having a grandma and she's put in the work to get to know him. My dad, well, he's chosen to ignore us. My mom had a health scare that made her realize life is short, but my dad is sticking to what he calls his "principles" and acting like we don't exist.

His loss.

After showering and dressing, I pack Abby's diaper bag and get everything piled into the family vehicle. Just as I walk back inside the house, I hear her stirring on the baby monitor. Thank the Lord she stayed napping while I got everything done. Most of the time, I'm not so fortunate.

I gather her into my arms. "Are you ready to go see your big brother graduate from high school?"

She grins, her chubby cheeks bunching with the movement.

"Oh, you can't wait to cheer for him?" I continue speaking. "Are you going to cry like me?"

She frowns as if not understanding my question.

"Don't worry, baby. He'll visit us on the weekends. Then again, Misha goes to George Mason too."

Abby's cheeks are back to a smile. No way she can truly understand just how much Taj and Misha are tethered together. Despite their year difference, they've been dating since Taj hit his junior year.

"Maybe the fact that Misha visits her folks means Taj will definitely come back. Don't they say mothers lose their sons to someone else's daughter?"

Abby giggles like that's the funniest notion. It's another thought that makes my heart pinch.

"Dear, sweet Abigail. Thank goodness we're a long way away from you dating."

"No, no, no. Abigail is never dating." Derrick walks into the nursery with a look of pure adoration on his face.

"What's that look for?" I shift Abby onto my hip now that she's all dressed in her graduation outfit.

"I have never seen anything as beautiful as you two ladies."

My cheeks heat, and I move forward into his embrace. He places a kiss on Abby's cheek. Her eyes light up, noticing her favorite person. I'm just the milk factory, but Derrick is her person. Taj is her second favorite.

"You ready to see our son walk across the stage?" Derrick asks.

I shake my head and blow out a breath. "No, but I have tissues in the diaper bag."

"I'll be there." Derrick drags a knuckle across my cheek. "We'll get through this."

"I hate change," I whine.

He kisses the tip of my nose. "I know, beautiful, but he'll be back to visit. As long as Misha keeps coming home to visit, he will too."

I laugh because isn't this what I told Abby earlier?

We head out, and soon we're seated in the stadium of Anchor Cove High to see our graduates. The band plays "Pomp and Circumstance" and the choir follows up with the national anthem. It's a normal graduation, but when they call for the graduates in the first row to stand, my heart begins to pound. Taj is an *A* and he's the last person in the first row. My hands start shaking as I turn my phone camera on.

"Give me Abby or the phone," my husband suggests.

I bite my lip then hand Derrick my cell in order to watch my child walk the stage uninhibited. I shout loudly when they call his name, though my voice breaks trying to suppress the sobs. He did it. I got him to this point.

When he was first born, getting to eighteen seemed so daunting. I had no choice but to take it one day at a time. Now that he's eighteen and a graduate, I want to rewind and go backward and have more time at other moments in his development. Even so, whatever the future holds for Taj, God has him. He's grown into a remarkable young man and I couldn't be prouder.

Derrick

I blink rapidly as Taj holds up his diploma and smiles our way. I'm taking a video, but Mrs. Avery is snapping photo after photo next to me. She's sniffling, Simone's crying silently, and Abby is babbling at the commotion. The Millers are sitting behind us whistling and Misha and her family are next to them cheering as well.

We're all so proud of Taj, but man, the house is going to feel empty with him gone during the school year. Thank goodness we have one last summer to be with him before he has to report to school in August.

After they make it through the rest of the graduates, Abigail starts fussing. I take her from Simone, and she settles down, nestling her head in the crook of my neck.

I love Simone. I love Taj. But nothing prepared me for the protectiveness that came over me when I got to hold Abigail for the very first time. This little girl has me wrapped around her finger. She's so loved by us all. Mrs. Avery is also thankful for a second chance to be a better grandparent than the last time. Though she's developing a great relationship with Taj, she has a completely clean slate with Abby.

We filter out of the stands and wait for Taj to come find us. We're throwing him a party in our backyard and I can't wait to see his face when he sees the car his mom and I bought for him. Before we left for the ceremony, I moved his new car from where it was hiding at one of Simone's rentals and parked it in the driveway, complete with a red bow on top.

Now we're all in the SUV with the others following close behind us.

"Mom, I can't believe you cried when they called my name," Taj says as we drive home.

"You watch your firstborn cross the stage and tell me you don't cry," Simone counters.

I grin at their antics.

"Dad, did you cry?" Taj asks, sitting behind me.

"Men don't cry," I joke.

"That's not true. You taught me that on our first youth camping trip."

"He has you there," Simone says.

"Well, I may have been misty-eyed, but no tears spilled down my face. Instead, I cleared my throat and told myself to wait until I take a shower tonight."

Simone and Taj laugh at my joke.

"Wait, what's that in the driveway?" Taj asks, cautious hope in his voice.

"Oh, that?" Simone smirks at her son. "Well, what does it look like?"

I put the car in Park and turn in my seat to get a look at his face. Taj's gaze darts from mine to Simone to mine to Simone's again.

"Happy graduation, son," Simone and I say simultaneously. We exchange glances and chuckle at each other.

"Wait, the car's mine?" Taj points to his chest.

Simone fishes keys out of her pocket then hands them to Taj. "We're so proud of you."

"Yo!" His mouth drops then he's out of the vehicle and exclaiming over the sedan in the driveway.

We get out and follow at a more sedate pace. Simone's got Abby in her arms when Taj whirls around and hugs her then kisses Abby on the cheek. Then he's hugging me tightly and I clasp my arm around the child of my heart.

"Love you, kid." Then I let go.

But Taj squeezes me tighter. "Love you more, Dad." He goes back to the car, removes the ribbon, and offers everyone a ride around the block. Misha's the only one who takes him up on the offer.

Our celebration is wonderful and lasts for a few hours before people slowly say goodbye. Finally, it's us three once again—Abby's already in her crib. Taj counts the money he got for gifts and looks at the Bible he got from Pastor David, who dropped in to congratulate him.

Simone's curled up on my side and we're sitting there listening as she recounts memories of Taj when he was younger.

He's got a smile on his face and then he sighs. "Mom, you know I'll be back to bug you every weekend."

"Don't say every weekend. Because one weekend, you'll want to hang out with new friends. One weekend, you'll want to do something with Misha. One weekend you'll want to fly and that's okay." She sniffs. "I don't want you to feel guilty if you start having your own life away from us. Just know we're here whenever you need us."

His Adam's apple bobs and he nods. "I love you, guys. Thank you for being the best mom and dad ever."

Okay, now I may actually tear up. I thank God for knowing what I needed before I ever knew myself.

Acknowledgments

Sometimes a book takes longer to write than I ever anticipated. I started writing this book back in 2024 and immediately loved the characters. But then life happened, and I had to set this aside. I was worried I wouldn't make it back to finish, but thankfully, I did. Unfortunately, when I picked it back up this year, it was after my own nana had passed.

So I want to send a heavenly thanks to Nana. Thank you for reading all of my books. For the times we sat next to each other to watch mysteries and read in our recliners. For the ways you showed me how spending time with God in the silence deepens our faith. I love you always.

Thank you also to my readers who put a personal stamp on *Anchor Cove*. To my friend, Debb Hackett, for naming Tidal Treats, and Tamesha Nolt for naming the town of Anchor Cove. To Sasha F. for the Avery name and Sherika M. for Simone's name.

A writer also couldn't get a story done without the critiques from her best critique partners. Andrea Boyd and Jaycee Weaver, thank you for all your comments and helping me believe in the story. Sarah Monzon, thank you so much for helping me brainstorm the ending! Y'all are the absolute best!

A special thank you to Carrie Schmidt for reading this in its infancy. Friend, there aren't enough words to let you know how much I appreciate you. Thank you for being such an encourager.

To my own hero, Glenn, I love you. If you'll notice there's a little bit of you in all my heroes and that's intentional. To my own boys who have slowly turned into young men faster than I've been ready. Isaiah, keep flying. Elijah, don't mind if I hold on a little bit tighter and a little bit longer. I love you, both!

About the Author

Toni Shiloh is a wife, mom, and an award-winning Christian contemporary romance author. Her novel *In Search of a Prince* won the first ever Christy Amplify award. It has been praised by Oprah Daily, POPSUGAR, Library Journal, and Booklist, and is a Parable Group bestseller. Her books have been finalists for the Holt Medallion and won a Selah Award. As a member of American Christian Fiction Writers (ACFW) and Faith, Hope & Love Christian Writers (FHLCW), Toni loves connecting with readers and authors alike via social media. Learn more at http://tonishiloh.com.

More Books by Toni Shiloh

Indie Novels

Series

Maple Run Series

Buying Love

Finding Love

Enduring Love

Risking Love

A Maple Run Christmas

Freedom Lake Series

Returning Home

Grace Restored

Finally Accepted

Faith & Fortune Series

The Trouble With Love

The Truth About Fame

The Price of Dreams

Novellas

A Proxy Wedding

More Books by Toni Shiloh

Deck the Shelves
A Snow White Christmas
An Ever After Summer
All the Moore
All I Want
Most Wonderful Time

Nonfiction

Warrior: How to Stand Firm in Everyday Suffering